Upper Elementary/
Junior Level
Textbook for Children

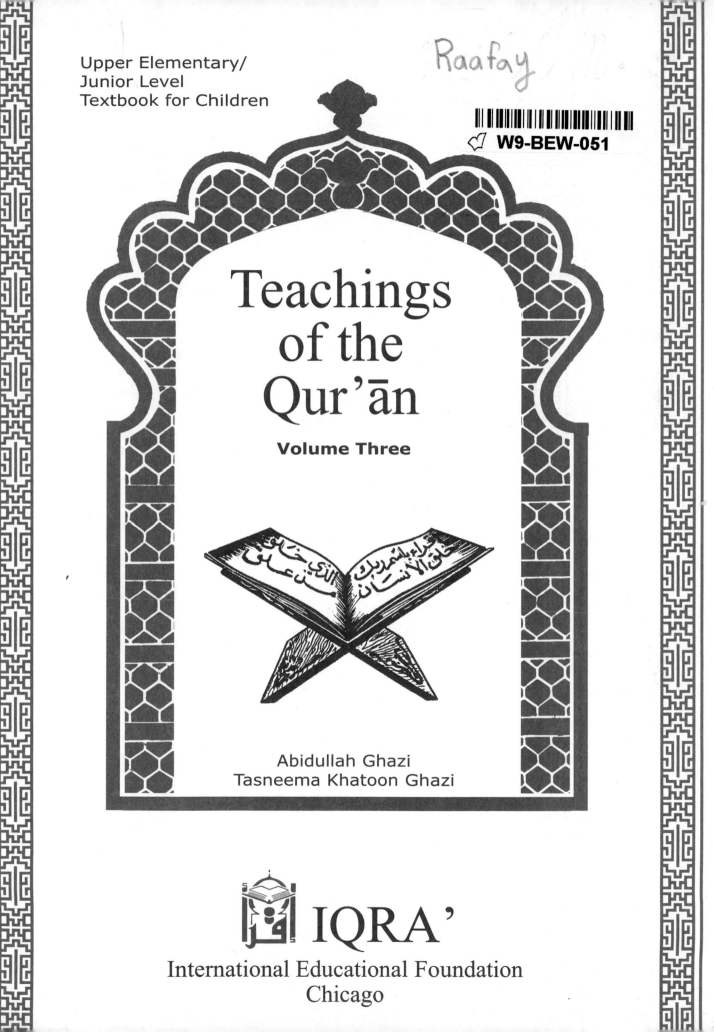

Teachings of the Qur'ān

Volume Three

Abidullah Ghazi
Tasneema Khatoon Ghazi

IQRA'
International Educational Foundation
Chicago

Part of a Comprehensive and Systematic Program of Islamic Studies

A Textbook for the
Program of Qur'ānic Studies
Upper Elementary Level/ Junior Level

Teachings of the Qur'ān,
Part 3

Chief Program Editors:

Abidullah al-Ansari Ghazi
Ph.D. History of Religion, Harvard University

Tasneema Khatoon Ghazi
Ph.D. Curriculum and Reading,
University of Minnesota

Reviewers:

Ghulam Haider Aasi
Ph.D. History of Islamic Religion,
Temple University

Fadel Abdallah
M.A. Islamic Studies,
University of Minnesota

Assad N. Busool
Ph.D. Arabic and Islamic Studies

Irfan Ahmad Khan
Ph.D. Philosophy, University of Illinois

Language Editors:

Suhaib Ghazi
University of Redlands,

Mahlaqa Patel
Student, University of Illinois Chicago

Carolyn Baugh
A.B. Duke Universtiy

Art Direction & Design:

Kathryn Heimberger
A.A.S. Electronic Design
American Academy of Art

Fourth printing October 2006
Printed in USA

Library of Congress Catalog Card Number 92-248962
ISBN # 1-56316-113-3

وَرَتِّلِ ٱلْقُرْءَانَ تَرْتِيلًا

"And recite the Qur'an in *Tartil*, slow and measured tone."
(*al-Muzammil* 73:4)

زَيِّنُوا القُرآنَ بِأَصْوَاتِكُمْ

"Beautify the Qur'an with your voices."
(Musnad Ahamd ibn Hanbal)

Dedicated to:

The Prominent Qur'an reciters of the early Generation of Muslims

Who spent their Life Practicing and Teaching the Art of *Tajwīd* and *Qira'ah*, the Recitation of the Qur'an in the most beautiful Manner

They Became the Founders of the Ten Schools of *Tajwīd* and *Qira'ah*

- Abdullah ibn Kathīr ad-Dārī (d. 120 A.H.)
- Nāfi' ibn 'Abd ar-Rahmān ibn Abi Na'īm (d 169)
- Abdullāh al-Hisabī (d. 118 A.H)
- Abu Amrū Zabban ibn al-Alā d.154 A.H.)
- Hamzah ibn Habib az-Zayyāt (d. 188 A.H)
- 'Asim ibn Abī An-Najūd al-Asadī (d. 137 A.H.)
- Abū Al-Hasan ' Ali ibn Hazah al-Kasā'i an-Nahwī (d.189 A.H)
- Ya'qub ibn Ishāq Hadramī (date unknown)
- Khalaf ibn Hishām (d.205 A.H.)
- Abū Ja'far Yazīd ibn al-Qa'qa' (d.130)

May Allah shower all of them with His Mercy!

All the these men derive their authority from Rasulul*lah (S)* through his Sahābah ®. Quoted in Muft*i Muhannmad Shaf*i', Ma'arif Al-Quran, pp. 16-17, Idara al-Ma'

TO PARENTS AND TEACHERS
(Read before you teach this textbook)

All praises are due to Allah ﷻ and choicest blessings be on Muhammad al-Mustafa, the final Messenger who came with the Final Revelation, the Qur'an, a light and guidance for all humankind.

IQRA' International Educational Foundation is grateful to Allah ﷻ for enabling it to do this unique work *Teachings of the Qur'an* (Volumes I, II & III) textbooks for Qur'anic Studies at elementary level. This is an attempt which is both unique in its presentation and thorough in its application. The three textbooks represent years of hard work in research and application of modern technology to present the teachings of the Qur'an to young children.

Teachings of the Qur'an, in three worldwide. The *Sīrah* Program is in use in Islamic schools in the USA and in most English speaking countries. It has also been translated into several languages.

Teachings of the Qur'an (I, II, III) along with companion volumes *Short Surāhs* and *Juz' 'Amma: 30* (parts I and II), represent the first systematic attempt to introduce the message of the Qur'an to elementary/junior age children at their own level and understanding.

IQRA's Comprehensive Program of Qur'anic Studies, like the Program of *Sīrah*, is produced at four levels and is under final editing and publication. The following points regarding these textbooks should be specially noted by the readers:

* These books are a part of IQRA's Comprehensive and Systematic Program of Islamic Studies at four levels; Preschool, Elementary, junior and senior. More than fifty scholars, educators and professionals are busy in producing this program. So far over seventy-five books have been completed. The complete program is expected to have over three hundred books; it will, *Inshā-Allah*, be the most comprehensive library of Islamic books and educational material for our children and youth. We expect its completion within the next five years, *Insha-Allah*.

* This volume (III) is divided into three sections and it deals with the teachings of the Qur'an on: Human Community, Muslims Community and Social Action.

* The vocabulary of the *'Ăyah*, now added to this volume, is provided at the end of the book as an appendix to help those students who want to further study the Qur'an through translation. Such an exercise would greatly facilitate both understanding and the Qur'an and learning Arabic. These books are also integral part of IQRA's comprehensive program of Arabic studies which aims to systematically teach Arabic as second language from an early age.

* Each lesson starts with an *'Ăyah*, which is selected to give the Messenger of the Qur'an on that subject. The *'Ăyah* is written in both Arabic and transliterated in English to help the child with the correct pronunciation. The meaning of the *'Ăyah* is provided in simple language.

* The message of the *'Ăyah* is then explained in short, simple sentences. The explanation covers not only the selected *'Ăyah* but the general theme of the Qur'an on that subject. The basic Message is repeated in three short sentences for the reinforcement under: WE HAVE LEARNED.

* A list of new and difficult words is given at the end of each lesson under: DO WE KNOW THESE WORDS

* A glossary of the words is provided at the end of the book. Workbooks based on the patterns of *Sīrah* program under publication is to provide reinforcement, practice and feedback.

* IQRA' International's efforts in the field of Islamic studies are unique, systematic and comprehensive. Very soon, we hope, the 'Ummah will realize its full importance and will benefit truly. *Inshā-Allah*, benefit from this endeavor. We urge you to join hands and remember us in your *Du'ā*, and support this worthy endeavor as *Sādāqāh Jariyāh* for you and your family.

May Allah ﷻ accept all our efforts!

The Chief Editors
IQRA' International Educational Foundation
7450 Skokie Blvd
Skokie IL 60077

May 20th, 2006
Rabi' al-Akhir 22, 1427

Table of Contents

بِسْمِ اللهِ الرَّحْمٰنِ الرَّحِيمِ

Table of Contents

Rules of Transliteration Islamic Invocations

بِسْمِ اللهِ الرَّحْمٰنِ الرَّحِيمِ

q	ق	*	z	ز	,	أ	*
k	ك		s	س		b	ب
l	ل		sh	ش		t	ت
m	م		ṣ	ص	*	th	ث	*
n	ن		ḍ	ض	*	j	ج	*
h	ه		ṭ	ط	*	ḥ	ح	*
w	و		z̧	ظ	*	kh	خ	*
y	ي		ʿ	ع	*	d	د	*
			gh	غ		dh	ذ	*
			f	ف		r	ر	

SHORT VOWELS	LONG VOWELS	DIPHTHONGS
a \ ـَ	a \ ـَا	aw \ ـَوْ
u \ ـُ	u \ ـُو	ai \ ـَيْ
i \ ـِ	i \ ـِي	

Such as: *kataba* كَتَبَ	Such as: *Kitab* كِتَاب	Such as: *Lawḥ* لَوْح
Such as: *Qul* قُلْ	Such as: *Mamnun* مَمْنُون	Such as: *'Ain* عَيْن
Such as: *Ni'mah* نِعْمَة	Such as: *Dīn* دِين	

* Special attention should be given to the symbols marked with stars for they have no equivalent in the English sounds.

Islamic Invocations

Rasūlullāh, *Ṣalla Allahu 'alaihi wa Sallam* (صَلَّى ٱللَّهُ عَلَيْهِ وَسَلَّم), and the Qur'ān teach us to glorify Allāh ﷻ when we mention His Name and to invoke His Blessings when we mention the names of His Angels, Messengers, the *Ṣaḥābah* and the Pious Ancestors.

When we mention the Name of Allāh we must say: *Subḥāna-hū Wa-Taʿālā* (سُبْحَانَهُ وَتَعَالَى), Glorified is He and High.

When we mention the name of Rasūlullāh ﷺ we must say: *Ṣalla Allāhu 'alai-hi wa-Sallam,* (صَلَّى ٱللَّهُ عَلَيْهِ وَسَلَّم), May Allāh's Blessings and Peace be upon him.

When we mention the name of an angel or a prophet we must say: *Alai-hi-(a)s-Salām* (عَلَيْهِ ٱلسَّلاَم), Upon him be peace.

When we hear the name of the *Ṣaḥābah* we must say:
For more than two, *Raḍiya-(A)llāhu Taʿālā 'an-hum,* (رَضِيَ ٱللَّهُ تَعَالَى عَنْهُمْ), May Allāh be pleased with them.
For two of them, *Raḍiya-(A)llāhu Taʿālā 'an-humā* (رَضِيَ ٱللَّهُ تَعَالَى عَنْهُمَا), May Allāh be pleased with both of them.
For a *Ṣaḥābī*, *Raḍiya-(A)llāhu Taʿālā 'an-hu* (رَضِيَ ٱللَّهُ تَعَالَى عَنْهُ), May Allāh be pleased with him.
For a *Ṣaḥābiyyah*, *Raḍiya-(A)llāhu Taʿālā 'an-hā* (رَضِيَ ٱللَّهُ تَعَالَى عَنْهَا), May Allāh be pleased with her.

When we hear the name of the Pious Ancestor *(As-Salaf as-Ṣāliḥ)* we must say
For a man, *Raḥmatu-(A)llāh 'alai-hi* (رَحْمَةُ ٱللَّهِ عَلَيْهِ), May Allāh's Mercy be upon him.
For a woman, *Raḥmatu-(A)llāh 'alai-hā* (رَحْمَةُ ٱللَّهِ عَلَيْهَا), May Allāh's Mercy be with her.

Section

I

The Human Community

The Human Family

بِسْمِ اللَّهِ الرَّحْمَٰنِ الرَّحِيمِ

يَٰٓأَيُّهَا ٱلنَّاسُ إِنَّا خَلَقْنَٰكُم مِّن ذَكَرٍ وَأُنثَىٰ وَجَعَلْنَٰكُمْ شُعُوبًا وَقَبَآئِلَ لِتَعَارَفُوٓا۟ إِنَّ أَكْرَمَكُمْ عِندَ ٱللَّهِ أَتْقَىٰكُمْ إِنَّ ٱللَّهَ عَلِيمٌ خَبِيرٌ

Yā'ayyuha-(a)n-nāsu'iannā khalaqnā-kum min dhakarin wa` unthā waj a'alnā-kum shu'ūban wa qabā'ila li-ta'ārafū'inna'akrama-kum 'ind(a)-Allahi'atqā-kum, 'inn(a)-Allaha'Alīmun Khabīr.

"Oh humankind! We have created you from a single (pair) of male and female, and made you into nations and tribes, that you may know each other, in fact, the most honored in the Sight of Allah is the one who is most righteous. Indeed! Allah is Knower and Well-Aware (of all things)."
(*Al-Hujurāt* 49:13)

EXPLANATION:

Allah ﷻ created all human beings from a single couple, one male, Prophet 'Ādam ﷺ, and one female, Hawwā' ﷺ. All of humankind is one family, and 'Ādam ﷺ and Hawwā' ﷺ are the parents of all humanity. Just as members of each family have many things in common, members of the human family also have many things in common with one another. And just as every family also has some differences, Allah ﷻ created different tribes, races, colors and language groups. All of this variation may make us look different, but we are still one big family.

It is natural for people who have common characteristics to feel more comfortable around each other. It is also natural for people who do not have common characteristics to feel uneasy or unsure about those outside their group. To be different does not mean one is better than others. Allah ﷻ created these differences so that we may try to know and understand each other.

Throughout history people developed ideas that because they were different from others, they are somehow better or superior than them. In considering themselves to be superior, they believed that others are inferior and unequal. Many stories have been invented to explain why some people are better than others. Often it is claimed that some people are special simply by the language they speak or the color of their skin. Many powerful races and cultures in the world developed social systems to their own advantage. Laws of untouchability were established that condemned certain people to be treated as unclean simply because they were born into a different group.

Islam condemns all of these ideas and it says that all human beings belong to the same family. All people are creations of One God. We are all children of 'Ādam ﷺ and Hawwā' ﵂ therefore, all of us are brothers and sisters. No individual is superior to any other individual, nor is any one group of people superior to any other group because of race, color, tribe, language and place of birth.

There are both good and bad in all groups of people. However, people are not good or bad because of their birth, but rather because of their actions. If one believes and behaves righteously, he or she is honored in the Sight of Allah ﷻ. Actions make people honorable or dishonorable and only Allah ﷻ knows who is more honored in His Sight.

The Qur'an teaches us that we must respect all people and treat them with justice and fairness. We should never prefer one people over another simply because of their color, language, tribe or nationality. Nor should we dishonor anyone because of these same factors.

We must never accept any racist thoughts which divide human beings into groups of inferior and superior. We must live virtuously and honor those who do good deeds regardless of the language they speak or the color of their skin. Muslims have a responsibility to show the Right Path to those who do not treat their fellow humans with respect.

WE HAVE LEARNED:

❖ Allāh ﷻ has created all human beings from a single couple, 'Ādam ﷺ and Hawwā' ﵂

❖ No one group of people is superior to any other because of color, tribe or race.

❖ The best people in the Sight of Allah ﷻ are those who are most righteous.

DO WE KNOW THESE WORDS?

inferior

superior

righteous

caste system

untouchability

Lesson 2

The Best Of Creations

بِسْمِ اللَّهِ الرَّحْمَٰنِ الرَّحِيمِ

لَقَدْ خَلَقْنَا ٱلْإِنسَٰنَ فِىٓ أَحْسَنِ تَقْوِيمٍ ۝

ثُمَّ رَدَدْنَٰهُ أَسْفَلَ سَٰفِلِينَ ۝

*Laqad khalaqnā-(a)l-insanā fi' ahsani taqwīm
Thummā radadnā-hu'asfala sāfīli`n*

"Surely, We have created humans in the best forms, then We reduce
them to the lowest (forms)."
(*at-Tīn 95*: 4-5)

EXPLANATION:

Allah ﷻ created everything. Allah ﷻ created all plants, animals and
human beings. The human beings are the best of Allah's creations. They
are called *'Ashraf al-Makhlūqāt* which means "Best of the Creations."

Human beings have been given the highest level of intelligence out of
all of God's creation. Only we have the freedom to do as we want. We
are the only creations that can choose to follow Allah's commands or to
reject them.

When people believe in Allah ﷻ and follow the teachings of His
prophets, they become the *'Ashraf al-Makhlūqāt*. They live their lives
peacefully and help others to do the same. These people are blessings for
all of humankind. They are the best examples of upright behavior.

However, people can also be the worst of Allah's creations. When they
reject Allah ﷻ and do not follow the teachings of His prophets, they
become the worst of creatures. These individuals follow the advice of
the *Shaitān* and create mischief on earth.

The worst of Allah's creations are those who do not respect other
people's rights. They steal other people's property, cheat in business and
create problems wherever they go. They care for no one but themselves
and their own interests. They may even go so far as to kill their fellow
human beings.

Muslims have been given the guidance of the Qur'an and the *Sunnah* of
Rasūlullāh ﷺ to follow. We have clear knowledge of what is right and
what is wrong. As Muslims, we have a responsibility before

Allah ﷻ to be the best examples of good behavior for others.

Allah ﷻ says in the Qur'an that only those people who have true faith and act virtuously are protected from being the worst of creations. For these people there are rewards in this life and the next.

❖ Human Beings are created as the best of Allah's creations.

❖ They can become the worst of His creations also.

❖ Through a Muslim's actions, he or she can be a blessing to him or herself, the community, and the entire human population.

DO WE KNOW THESE WORDS?

Ashraf al-Makhlūqāt

Shaitān

بِسْمِ اللهِ الرَّحْمَٰنِ الرَّحِيمِ

أَلَّا تَزِرُ وَازِرَةٌ وِزْرَ أُخْرَىٰ ۝ وَأَن لَّيْسَ لِلْإِنسَٰنِ إِلَّا مَا سَعَىٰ ۝ وَأَنَّ سَعْيَهُ سَوْفَ يُرَىٰ ۝ ثُمَّ يُجْزَىٰهُ الْجَزَاءَ الْأَوْفَىٰ ۝

Al-lā taziru wāziratun wizra'ukhra. Wa'an laisa li(a)l-'insani'illā mā sa'ā. Wa'anna-sa'ya-hu sawfa yurā. Thumma yujzā-hu-(a)l-jazā'a(a)l-'awfā.

"That no bearer of burden shall bear the burden of another. That a human achieves only what he makes an effort for. And that his effort shall be seen. The he shall be rewarded for it with a full reward."
(an-Nājm 53: 38-41)

EXPLANATION:

Allah ﷻ made humans as the *'Ashraf al-Makhlūqāt* and gave them the choice and the wisdom to choose between good and evil. Every individual must decide which path to follow in life. The messengers of Allah taught people to believe in Allah ﷻ and to behave virtuously. However, everyone is given a choice to choose between the path of righteousness and the path of *Shaitān*.

In this life people are free to choose between good and evil. We are free to live our lives as we wish. In the Hereafter we will be judged according to how we chose to live life in this world. Everyone will receive the rewards of his or her actions. No one will be punished for the crime of another.

One of Allah's names is *al-Ādil*, which means "the Just." He judges everyone with complete justice. He is also *ar-Rahmān*, the Mercy-Giving and *ar-Rahīm*, the Merciful. His doors of mercy are always open to everyone.

When a person commits an evil action, Allah ﷻ gives that person a chance to seek forgiveness and return to the straight path. Allah ﷻ is *al-Ādil* and does not punish a person for a sin that he or she has not committed nor does He punish anyone for the sins that others have committed.

Many cultures and civilizations in the past used to punish people for the faults of others. They also had different punishments for different types of people. There was one kind of justice for the free person and another for the slave. They treated the rich differently from the poor. But Allah's justice is the same for everyone. The laws of Islam treat every human being with equal justice.

Everyone will see the results of his or her actions both in this world and in the Hereafter. Allah ﷻ rewards everyone for his or her own efforts. A person must make a sincere effort to do good. Sometimes we do not seem to be getting any reward of our good actions and we feel frustrated. A Muslim is one who does not give up hope. Allah ﷻ advises us:

$$\text{لَا تَقۡنَطُوا۟ مِن رَّحۡمَةِ ٱللَّهِ ۚ إِنَّ ٱللَّهَ يَغۡفِرُ ٱلذُّنُوبَ جَمِيعًا ۚ إِنَّهُۥ هُوَ ٱلۡغَفُورُ ٱلرَّحِيمُ ۝}$$

"Do not lose hope in the Mercy of Allah, for Allah forgives all sins. He is Oft-Forgiving, Most Merciful."
(az-Zumar 39:53)

If sometimes we feel that our prayers are not answered and our efforts unrewarded, it is because Allah ﷻ has something better to offer. For some prayers and hard work He reserves the reward for 'Ākhirāh. And the reward of the 'Ākhirāh is always a much greater reward than in this life.

Original Sin

Some religions have a different view of the forgiveness of sins than Islam. For instance Christianity teaches a concept called "Original Sin." According to this idea 'Ādam ﷺ caused all of his descendents to be born in natural state of disobedience because he ate the forbidden fruit. God will not forgive this condition without a sacrifice. This sacrifice came in the form of Jesus Christ, whom Christians consider to be the actual son of God. By giving his life as a sacrifice on the cross, Jesus became the mediator between humans and God. No matter what a person does that is good and righteous, he or she can be forgiven only by believing in Jesus' sacrifice on the cross.

Such and idea is not accepted within the teachings of Islam. According to the Qur'an, 'Ādam ﷺ did commit a sin by eating from the forbidden fruit. However, he immediately realized his mistake and asked Allah ﷻ for forgiveness. Allah ﷻ is Forgiving and Merciful and He forgave 'Ādam ﷺ for his mistake. Allah ﷻ is al-'Ādil, the Just and He does not punish anyone for the sins of another. Also Islam teaches that Jesus was a great prophet, but no more than a man. It also believes that Jesus was not killed on the cross.

WE HAVE LEARNED:

❖ Allāh ﷻ is Just and Forgiving.

❖ He rewards and punishes people according to their actions.

❖ Allāh ﷻ never punishes a person for the sins of another person.

DO WE KNOW THESE WORDS?

'Ādil

atom's weight

bearer of burden

Original Sin

Changing From Within

بِسْمِ اللّٰهِ الرَّحْمٰنِ الرَّحِيمِ

إِنَّ ٱللَّهَ لَا يُغَيِّرُ مَا بِقَوْمٍ حَتَّىٰ يُغَيِّرُواْ مَا بِأَنفُسِهِمْ

*'Inn(a)-Allaha lā yughayyiru mā bi-qawmin
hattā yughayyirū mā bi-'anfusi-him*

"Indeed! Never will Allah change the condition of people,
unless they change it (from within) themselves."
(*ar-Ra'd* 13:11)

EXPLANATION:

Everything in the universe follows Allah's commands and laws. We see these laws in everyday life all the time. Some of these laws that affect all human beings are the rising and setting of the sun, the change of seasons, and life and death. Another name for these laws is *Sunnat Allah*, the order of Allah ﷻ. Everything in existence follows these laws.

Human beings have a special advantage over all other creations. They can discover these laws and use them to their advantage. However, they can also work against these laws and bring disaster upon themselves.

One of the laws of Allah ﷻ is that everyone must work hard to achieve what they desire. Communities and nations must also work hard to improve themselves. People must change from within in order to change their outside condition. Changing from within means working to make our beliefs, our attitudes and our thinking in tune with the teachings of Islam. Rasulūllāh ﷺ said:

"One's actions are determined by one's intentions.
Everyone is rewarded for what he or she intends."
(*al-Bukhārī*)

This means that righteous actions must start with righteous intentions. Everyone must strive to get what he or she wants, but our striving must be with a correct attitude.

If we try to achieve what we want without changing from within we may act wrongly. We may break the law or decide to do *Harām* things. Instead of working hard to achieve what we want we may intentionally or unintentionally take it by stealing or cheating.

Muslims are commanded to work for this world as well as for the 'Ākhirāh. They must make a serious and sincere effort to achieve a better life here in this world and use it for the 'Ākhirāh.

We must remember that Islam teaches us that:

- ❖ We must have righteous beliefs and attitudes before we can act to achieve our goals.
- ❖ When we change from within and work righteously, Allāh ﷻ will certainly help us.

Allāh ﷻ commands us to work hard and ask Him for the reward of both worlds:

$$رَبَّنَآ ءَاتِنَا فِى ٱلدُّنْيَا حَسَنَةً وَفِى ٱلْأَخِرَةِ حَسَنَةً وَقِنَا عَذَابَ ٱلنَّارِ ۝$$

"Oh Lord! Give us good in this world and good in the Hereafter and save us from the punishment of the Fire."
(al-Baqarah 2:201)

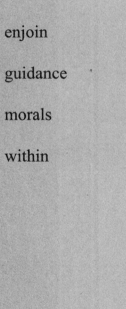

WE HAVE LEARNED:

- ❖ Allāh ﷻ does not help those who do not help themselves.

- ❖ Everyone is rewarded for their good work in this world.

- ❖ The reward of the 'Ākhirāh is only for the Believers.

DO WE KNOW THESE WORDS?

enjoin

guidance

morals

within

بِسْمِ اللَّهِ الرَّحْمَنِ الرَّحِيمِ

وَتَعَاوَنُواْ عَلَى ٱلْبِرِّ وَٱلتَّقْوَىٰ ۖ وَلَا تَعَاوَنُواْ عَلَى ٱلْإِثْمِ وَٱلْعُدْوَٰنِ ۚ

*Wa taʿāwanū ʿala-(a)l-birri wa-(a)t-taqwā
wa-lā taʿāwanū ʿala-(a)l-ʿithmi wa-(a)l-ʿudwān*

"And help each other in goodness and piety and do
Not cooperate with one another in sin and aggression."
(*al-Māʾidah 5:2*)

EXPLANATION:

We live in society with other people. We are all connected to each other as relatives, friends, neighbors, classmates and fellow citizens. All of us need each other and we must work together to do those things that are good for everyone and to stop what harms everyone.

Members of our families must work together to make their household successful. At school, the principal, teachers, and students all work together to run their school efficiently. In a town or city the mayor, city council members, the police force, the fire department and the citizens cooperate to make their city run smoothly.

In a similar way, everyone must cooperate with one another to make the world a better place. Most people want to live peacefully and work with others for the common good. However there are some people who do not respect the rules of society and the rights of others. These people commit evil acts against not only themselves but also against society. Communities have to work together to stop such trouble makers and, if possible, guide them to goodness.

Allah ﷻ commands us to cooperate with other people in all those things that are good. In doing so, we make our society a better place for everyone. Allah ﷻ does not want us to cooperate with those who carry out wrong and sinful acts.

The Qurʾan teaches us what is good and right, and it tells us what is sinful and wrong. Generally most cultures around the world agree on what kinds of actions are good and what kinds are wrong. Countries and

10

communities make laws to encourage good and to forbid evil. We Muslims have a special responsibility to work with everyone regardless of their race, language or religion to make society a better place to live in.

In many non-Muslims societies, things that are forbidden by Allah ﷻ, such as drinking, gambling and dating, are considered acceptable and are permitted by the laws of the land. However as Muslims we know what is allowed by Allah ﷻ and what is forbidden by Him. We must be sure that we do not participate in those activities which are clearly forbidden.

Most people in our nation respect other people's beliefs and actions. We have special responsibility to inform others about the beliefs of Islam. Informing others about our religion and its practices is the best form of *Da'wah*.

If we live in a society where others do not respect our beliefs and practices, we still must conform to Allah's guidance. Allah ﷻ is our Protector and Lord. When we know what is true and what is correct and follow it even if it is difficult to do so, Allah ﷻ will guide us and makes things easy for us.

If we live in a society where most people are Muslim and yet it is a society which does not follow codes of Islamic *'Akhlāq*, we must work together with other beleivers to make that society a better place.

To promote good in every society and in all situations we must work together with others.

WE HAVE LEARNED:

❖ We must cooperate with others in doing those things that are good and permitted by Allāh ﷻ

❖ We must not participate in those things that are evil and forbidden by Allāh ﷻ

❖ We must work together to make our society a better place for all.

DO WE KNOW THESE WORDS?

cooperate

piety

promote

society

No Compulsion In Religion

بِسْمِ اللَّهِ الرَّحْمَٰنِ الرَّحِيمِ

لَآ إِكْرَاهَ فِى الدِّينِ ۖ قَد تَّبَيَّنَ الرُّشْدُ مِنَ الْغَيِّ

Lā'ikrāha fi-(a)d-dīni qad tabayyana-(a)r-rushdu min al-ghayyi...

"There is no compulsion in religion; the right
Path is made clear from error."
(*al-Baqarah* 2: 256)

EXPLANATION:

Throughout history Allah ﷻ has sent many messengers to the peoples of the world. All of them brought the religion of Islam to the people to whom they were sent. These messengers taught their people to follow the path of submission to the One God and to avoid the advice of *Shaiṭān*.

All through the world we can find many religions. Allah ﷻ commands Muslims to invite everyone to follow the way of Islam. But Allah ﷻ does not want us to *force* others to accept the message of Islam. Allah ﷻ gives people the freedom to believe in whatever they wish. We cannot change other people's ways of thinking by force. To convince someone one of the good qualities of a belief you have to present your views in a respectable manner and offer ideas clearly and patiently. Real guidance, as Allah ﷻ says, is in His hands alone.

Islam does not allow us to make changes in our religion. Islam is a complete as Allah ﷻ revealed it. We do not believe that any compromise in religion is possible. But we must support the rights of other people to follow their own religions or ideas. The Qurān says:

لَكُمْ دِينُكُمْ وَلِيَ دِينِ ۖ

"You have your religion and I have my religion."
(*al-Kāfirūn* 109: 6)

Even though Islam teaches us *Tawhīd,* Allah ﷻ forbids us to make fun of the idols and images that some people worship. As Muslims, we have a responsibility to inform these people about *Tawhīd,* the belief in One God, not many; but we should not mock their beliefs and make fun of what they worship. Violence against others because of their beliefs is intolerable in Islam.

The Qur'an teaches us:

وَلَا تَسُبُّوا۟ ٱلَّذِينَ يَدْعُونَ مِن دُونِ ٱللَّهِ فَيَسُبُّوا۟ ٱللَّهَ عَدْوًۢا بِغَيْرِ عِلْمٍ ۗ كَذَٰلِكَ زَيَّنَّا لِكُلِّ أُمَّةٍ عَمَلَهُمْ ثُمَّ إِلَىٰ رَبِّهِم مَّرْجِعُهُمْ فَيُنَبِّئُهُم بِمَا كَانُوا۟ يَعْمَلُونَ ۝

"Do not curse (call bad names) those on whom they call for help (worship) besides Allah, in case, because of their ignorance, they curse Allah out of enmity; thus We have made to each people their actions attractive, then to their Lord shall they return, and He will tell Them of what they were doing."
(al-'An'ām 6: 108)

Since we live in a world in which different people follow different faiths, we must live peacefully with each other. As we read in the previous lessons, Allah ﷻ wants Muslims to cooperate with all peoples in doing what is right and avoid participating in the things that are wrong.

The Qur'an especially commands Muslims to cooperate with The People of the Book (Christians and Jews) in doing those things that their religions have in common with Islam:

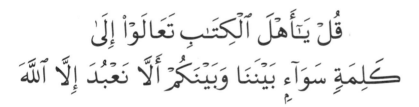

"O People of the Book! Come to what is common between us and you, that we shall worship none but God."
('Āl 'Imrān 3: 64)

As Muslims, we must follow our faith sincerely, make Da'wah to invite others to Islam in a pleasant manner, and respect the beliefs of others.

WE HAVE LEARNED:

❖ There is no force or compulsion used to convert others to Islām.

❖ We must make *Da'wah* in a clear and peaceful manner.

❖ We must respect other peoples' faith and leave their guidance to Allāh ﷻ

DO WE KNOW THESE WORDS?

Da'wah

conversion

faith

People of the Book

compel

بِسْمِ اللَّهِ الرَّحْمَنِ الرَّحِيمِ

وَهُوَ ٱلَّذِى جَعَلَكُمْ خَلَـٰٓئِفَ ٱلْأَرْضِ
وَرَفَعَ بَعْضَكُمْ فَوْقَ بَعْضٍ دَرَجَـٰتٍ لِّيَبْلُوَكُمْ فِى مَآ ءَاتَىٰكُمْ

*Wa huw(a)-Alladhi ja'ala-kum khalā'ifa (a)l-ardi wa rafa'a
ba'da-kum fawqa ba'din darajātin li-yabluwa-kum fī mā 'atā-kum*

"He it is Who has appointed you as the *Khulafā* (Viceroys) of the
Earth and has exalted some of you in rank over others, that He
may try you by that which He has given you."
(*al-'An'ām* 6:165)

EXPLANATION:

Allah ﷻ made human beings *'Ashraf al-Makhlūqāt* and has appointed
them to be His *Khulafā'* (Viceroys) on Earth. Being a *Khalīfah* of Allah
ﷻ is a serious responsibility and a special gift. We must follow Allah's
Guidance in all aspects of our lives. The Qur'an informs us:

إِنَّا عَرَضْنَا ٱلْأَمَانَةَ عَلَى ٱلسَّمَـٰوَٰتِ وَٱلْأَرْضِ
وَٱلْجِبَالِ فَأَبَيْنَ أَن يَحْمِلْنَهَا وَأَشْفَقْنَ مِنْهَا وَحَمَلَهَا ٱلْإِنسَـٰنُ

"Indeed! We offered this trust to the Heavens and the
Earth and the hills, but they refused to undertake it, and
were afraid of it, but humanity accepted it..."
(*al-'Ahzāb* 33: 72)

It is due to the acceptance of this trust that Allah ﷻ has made humans
His *Khulafā'* on Earth. As *Khulafā'*, we have an obligation to follow
Allah's commands. Allah ﷻ created everything in heaven and earth for
our use:

وَسَخَّرَ لَكُم مَّا فِى ٱلسَّمَـٰوَٰتِ وَمَا فِى ٱلْأَرْضِ جَمِيعًا مِّنْهُ

"And He has made to serve you
All that is on Heaven and on Earth."
(*al-Jāthiyah* 45: 13)

As human beings whom Allah ﷻ has blessed with intelligence, each one of us is responsible for our actions. As *Khulafā'* we must practice justice and share equally and fairly with others all the blessings that Allah ﷻ has placed in our trust. We must also preserve these blessings and gifts for those who will come after us.

Allah ﷻ tells us:

$$كُلُواْ وَٱشْرَبُواْ وَلَا تُسْرِفُواْ إِنَّهُ لَا يُحِبُّ ٱلْمُسْرِفِينَ$$

"Eat and drink, but do not be wasteful.
For Allah does not love the wasteful."
(al-A'rāf 7:31)

As *Khulafā* we must act as caretakers of our world and not waste its resources. All the resources of the planet are the gifts of Allah ﷻ for all humanity. These resources belong not only to those who are living, but also to those who are not yet born. All of Earth's blessings are both His gifts to us as well as a test of our responsibility. Yet all of us often take these gifts for granted and waste them.

We can be wasteful in many ways:

❖ We may carelessly waste what is in excess of our needs.
❖ We may not make proper use of all the blessings that Allah ﷻ has given to us.
❖ We may destroy Allah's gifts out of greed or carelessness.
❖ We do not share Allah's gifts which have been placed in our trust.

As *Khulafā* we must use everything carefully without abusing our authority or wasting precious resources.

WE HAVE LEARNED:

❖ Human beings have been created as Allāh's ﷻ *Khulafā* on this Earth.

❖ We have a responsibility to follow Allāh's ﷻ Commands and make proper use of the resources that He has provided for us.

❖ We should enjoy Allāh's ﷻ Blessings but we must not waste them.

DO WE KNOW THESE WORDS?

bounties

carelessness

resources

wastefulness

بِسْمِ اللَّهِ الرَّحْمَٰنِ الرَّحِيمِ

قُلْ مَنْ حَرَّمَ زِينَةَ ٱللَّهِ ٱلَّتِىٓ أَخْرَجَ لِعِبَادِهِۦ وَٱلطَّيِّبَٰتِ مِنَ ٱلرِّزْقِ

Qul man harrama zīnata-(A)llāhi (a)llatī'akhraja li-'ibādihī
Wa- (a)ṭṭayibāti mina (a)r- rizq(i)...

"Say! Who has forbidden the beautiful things of Allah that He has created for His servants, and the things, clean and pure which He has provided for support..."
(al-'A'rāf 7: 32)

قُلْ إِنَّمَا حَرَّمَ رَبِّىَ ٱلْفَوَٰحِشَ مَا ظَهَرَ مِنْهَا وَمَا بَطَنَ وَٱلْإِثْمَ وَٱلْبَغْىَ بِغَيْرِ ٱلْحَقِّ وَأَن تُشْرِكُوا۟ بِٱللَّهِ مَا لَمْ يُنَزِّلْ بِهِۦ سُلْطَٰنًا وَأَن تَقُولُوا۟ عَلَى ٱللَّهِ مَا لَا تَعْلَمُونَ ۝

*Qul' innamā harrama Rabbiya (a)l-fawahisha mā zahara
min-hā wa mā batana wa (a)l-'ithma wa (a)l-baghya bighairi
(a)l-haqqi wa 'an tushrikū bi (A)llāhi mā lam yunnazzil bi-hī
sulatānāh, wa an taqūlu 'ala (A)llāhi mā lā ta'lamūn.*

"Say the things that my Lord has really forbidden are: shameful deeds, whether open or secret, sins, wrongful oppression against truth and reason, and that you accept partners with Allah for which He has given no authority, and that you say concerning Allah that you do not know."
(al-'A'rāf 7: 33)

EXPLANATION:

Allah ﷻ has made certain things *Halāl* in this world that He has permitted us to use. He has also made certain things *Harām* that He has forbidden us to use. As believers we are expected to follow Allah's Commands and accept the *Halāl* and avoid the *Harām*. No one has a right to make *Halāl* things *Harām* or *Harām* things *Halāl*. All *Halāl* things are beautiful even though their beautiful qualities we may sometimes not see. All *Halāl* things are made pure and clean by Allah ﷻ.

Allah ﷻ has forbidden those things which are shameful, wrong, and unclean and which may lead to *shirk*. Allah ﷻ has made His Commands clear in the Qur'an and Rasūlullāh ﷺ further explained them through

16

his *Sunnah*. Rasūlullāh ﷺ advises us that:

> "Whatever Allah has made obligatory do not disobey it. Wherever Allah has set limitations, do not cross them. He has made certain things *Harām*, do not engage in them. He has been silent about certain things, because of His Mercy to you, without forgetting them, do not go after them."
>
> (ad-Dār Quṭni)

Among the *Harām* (forbidden) things to eat are:

The meat of any product made of an animal which is forbidden (such as pig or carnivores).

Any animal or bird that is permissible but not slaughtered in the Islamic way *of Dhabī*hah. The slaughtered meat of The People of the Book is allowed, but that *of a Mushriks* is not permitted.

The meat of any already dead animal or bird; the blood of any creature; all intoxicating drinks or drugs; and all things that are *Najas*, ritually impure, such as urine, feces, vomit etc.

It is also important for the believers that they earn their living lawfully through permi*tted* (*Halāl*) work, rightful inheritance, and busine*ss* in *Halāl* things. We are not permitted to steal, cheat, accept bribes, gamble and take unlawful possession of other's wealth. We can find details o*f the Halāl and Harām* in Fiqh books.

Islam permits us to enjoy the beautiful things of the world that have been created by Allah ﷻ. We must always be moderate and responsible in the use of things that Allah ﷻ permitted. We must avoid being wasteful. We must accept the limitations of the Harām as set by Allah ﷻ and avoid them at every cost.

There is a *great Barakah in Halāl*, though it may be small and no *Barakah in Harām* though it may be plentiful.

WE HAVE LEARNED:

❖ The limits of *Halāl* and *Harām* are set by Allāh ﷻ and explained by the *Sunnah* of Rasūlullāh ﷺ

❖ A believer must always eat and drink out of *Halāl* foods and drinks.

❖ A believer must always earn his living through *Halāl* means.

DO WE KNOW THESE WORDS?

Dhabīhah

intoxicant

moderate

Najas

Halāl

Harām

Do Not Kill

بِسۡمِ اللهِ الرَّحۡمٰنِ الرَّحِيۡمِ

أَنَّهُۥ مَن قَتَلَ نَفۡسَۢا بِغَيۡرِ نَفۡسٍ أَوۡ فَسَادٍ فِى ٱلۡأَرۡضِ فَكَأَنَّمَا قَتَلَ ٱلنَّاسَ جَمِيعًۭا وَمَنۡ أَحۡيَاهَا فَكَأَنَّمَآ أَحۡيَا ٱلنَّاسَ جَمِيعًۭا

*...'Anna-hū man qatala nafsan gi-ghairi
nafsin 'aw fasāsadin fi(a)l-'ardi fa-ka-'annamā
qatala-n-nāsa jamī 'an, wa-man'ahyā ha fa-ka-'annamā
'ahyā-n-nāsa jamī'ā...*

"... that if anyone killed a person – unless it be for
Murder or for spreading mischief in the
Land – it would be as if he killed the whole of
Humankind. And if anyone saved a life it
Would be as if he saved the life of the whole of humankind."
(*al-Mā'idah* 5:32)

EXPLANATION:

The life of every human being is sacred in Islam. Muslims and non-Muslims, rich and poor, adults and children all have the right to live. No human being has the right to take the life of another human being on purpose. Even governments do not have the right to take life of an innocent person.

Those people who kill others, commit crimes against other human beings, spread mischief and break laws must be punished by society. Such people must be tried by a court of law and they should be allowed to defend themselves.

Islam wants fairness and equal justice for all. In some societies, people feel one must be lenient with those who kill or break other laws. Some societies oppose capital punishment for murderers. Capital punishment is the most serious form of punishment since it involves execution of the criminal. Yet by not punishing criminals, one shows injustice and unfairness to the victims of crime. Justice means protecting the innocent and weak while punishing the guilty and oppressors.

Killing an innocent person is a very serious crime in Islam. The Qur'an says:

$$\text{وَلَا تَقْتُلُوا۟ ٱلنَّفْسَ ٱلَّتِى حَرَّمَ ٱللَّهُ إِلَّا بِٱلْحَقِّ}$$

"And do not take life that Allah has made sacred, except for the right (reasons)."
(al-'Isrā 17: 33)

Some people feel they can do whatever they want with their children. Some parents used to kill their children because they could not afford to take care of them. Some people in the past used to sacrifice their children to the idols they worshiped as gods. Before the coming of Islam the Arabs used to bury their daughters alive because they didn't want female children.
Allah ﷻ absolutely forbids all crimes against children:

$$\text{وَلَا تَقْتُلُوٓا۟ أَوْلَٰدَكُمْ خَشْيَةَ إِمْلَٰقٍ نَّحْنُ نَرْزُقُهُمْ وَإِيَّاكُمْ}$$

"And do not kill your children, fearing poverty:
We shall provide for them as We do for you."
(al-'Isrā 17: 31)

Islam teaches us that the life of one person is as important as the life of all others. Therefore Allah ﷻ established the principle that anyone who kills an innocent person is equal to killing all of humanity. Likewise, anyone who has saved the life of one person has saved the life of all humanity.

Any society which prefers one people over another based on race, color, culture or language is unjust. Killing someone based on these considerations is even more unjust. If any society allows this injustice the entire society suffers. Islam absolutely forbids this.

The Qur'an is the world's first constitution to introduce the idea of human rights. The term "Human rights" means that all people have certain basic rights which must be protected and respected by the law. Nowadays many states have human rights recognized in their laws.

Everyone in the society has a duty to save the lives of other human beings. Saving others' lives includes making laws that protect the innocent and punish those people who break the law or show disrespect for life. Societies must also be ready to offer help to those who are in danger. In societies where the rule of law is respected by the majority of the people, everyone can live freely and peacefully.

19

WE HAVE LEARNED:

❖ Killing an innocent human being is completely forbidden in Islām.

❖ Saving the life of one person is like saving the life of all people.

❖ The Qur'ān is the first written constitution which recognizes the rights of all human beings.

DO WE KNOW THESE WORDS?

caste

constitution

human rights

humanity

recognize

society

The Law Of Equality

بِسْمِ اللهِ الرَّحْمَنِ الرَّحِيمِ

وَلَكُمْ فِى ٱلْقِصَاصِ حَيَوٰةٌ
يَٰٓأُو۟لِى ٱلْأَلْبَٰبِ لَعَلَّكُمْ تَتَّقُونَ ﴿١٧٩﴾

Wa- la-kum fi-(a)l- qisāsi hayātun yā' uli-(a)l-'albābi la ' alla-kum tattaqūn(a)

"In the law of equality, there is (a saving of) life to you, Oh People of understanding, that you may restrain yourself."
(*al-Baqarah* 2:179)

EXPLANATION:

Islam believes in justice and it allows those who have been wronged to seek compensation for the wrong done against them. If someone kills an innocent person, the right of recompense is given to the murdered person's relatives. This means that these relatives have a right to see that the murderer is either executed or that they receive just monetary compensation. This right is carried out against the guilty person only – not his family.

Although forgiveness may be preferred at times, the relatives of the murdered have the right to choose to forgive or not. To forgive people is, no doubt, a righteous thing, but we cannot make it a law to always forgive criminals. To set lawbreakers (especially violent ones) free means to endanger the lives of more innocent people. The Qur'an teaches us that sometimes by taking the life of an offender the lives of many people are saved.

The Qur'an wants criminals to know that crime does not pay. It wants innocent people to know that they have full protection under Islamic law. Everyone has equal rights under Islamic law, whether they are weak or strong, poor or rich, Muslim or non-Muslim.

Allah ﷻ says in the Qur'an:

أَنَّهُ مَن قَتَلَ نَفْسًا بِغَيْرِ نَفْسٍ أَوْ فَسَادٍ فِي ٱلْأَرْضِ فَكَأَنَّمَا قَتَلَ ٱلنَّاسَ جَمِيعًا وَمَنْ أَحْيَاهَا فَكَأَنَّمَآ أَحْيَا ٱلنَّاسَ جَمِيعًا

"…If anyone kills a person – unless it be for murder
or for spreading mischief in the land, it would
be as if he has killed the whole people."
(*al-Mā'idah* 5:32)

By executing murderers, we save society from further danger from these individuals, because many times murderers murder again and again if not permanently stopped. If criminals know that the laws of society are lenient and that they will be out of prison shortly after being sent to into it, they will be encouraged to commit more crimes. In such situations the law fails to protect the innocent.

WE HAVE LEARNED:

❖ Islām gives the right of equality to the relatives of the innocent person who was killed.

❖ By taking the life of a guilty person, we can save the lives of many innocent people.

❖ Many times freeing a criminal endangers the lives of the innocent.

DO WE KNOW THESE WORDS?

compensation

guilty

innocent

retaliation

recompense

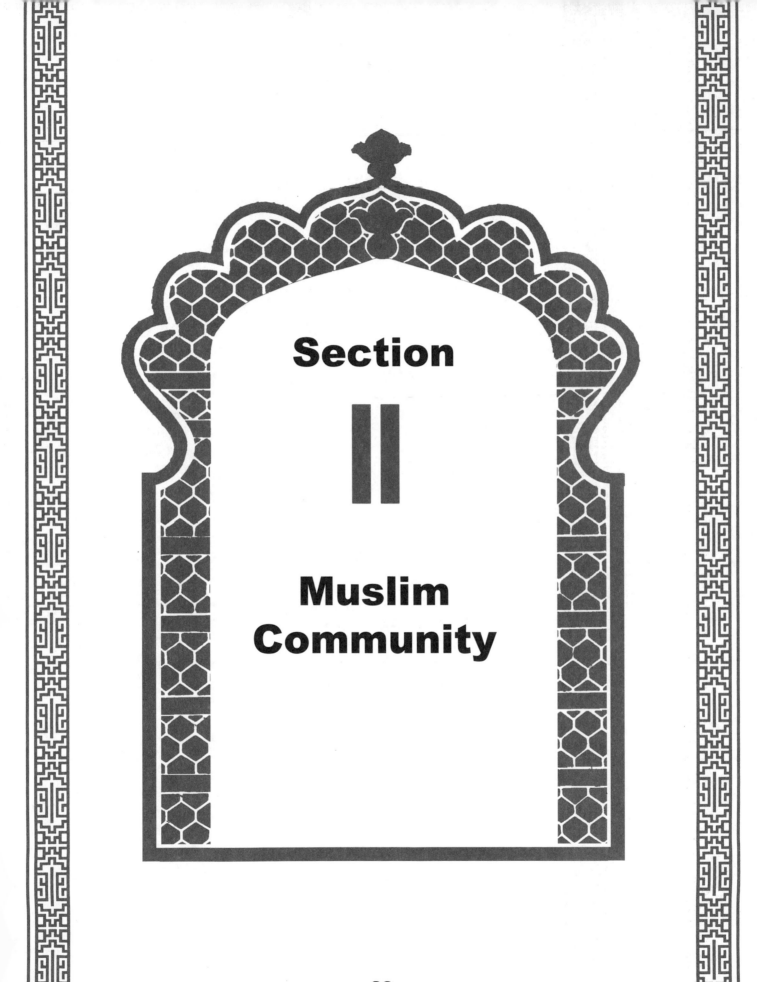

Section

II

Muslim Community

بِسۡمِ ٱللَّهِ ٱلرَّحۡمَٰنِ ٱلرَّحِيمِ

يَٰٓأَيُّهَا ٱلَّذِينَ ءَامَنُوا۟ ٱتَّقُوا۟ ٱللَّهَ حَقَّ تُقَاتِهِۦ وَلَا تَمُوتُنَّ إِلَّا وَأَنتُم مُّسۡلِمُونَ ﴿١٠٢﴾

*Yā' ayyuha-(a)lladhīna' āmanū-(a)t-taqu-(A)llāha haqqa tuqāti-hī
wa-lā tamūtunna' illā wa-'antum Muslimūn*

"O Believers! Have *Taqwā* (God-consciousness) of Allah as much as is
due to Him, and do not die unless you are Muslims."
(*Āl 'Imrān* 3:102)

EXPLANATION:

Allah ﷻ wants Muslims to be firm believers and have *Taqwā*. *Taqwā*
means to love Allah ﷻ, to be conscious of Him and to fear Him. *Taqwā*
means doing those things that are *Halāl* and not doing those things that
are *Harām*. One who has *Taqwā* is called a *Muttaqī*.

Taqwā brings us closer to Allah ﷻ and to the *Sunnah* of Rasūlallah ﷺ
. By bringing us closer to the teachings of the Qur'an, *Taqwā* makes it
easy for us to follow the Straight Path.

Taqwā means to accept Islam completely. A Muslim must remain true to
his or her faith and steadfast in his or her actions at all times. We cannot
choose to be a Muslim at one time, when it is most convenient for us,
and be a non-Muslim at other times. We cannot decide to believe in only
some parts of Islam and leave other parts out.

It is important that we always live as Muslims and die as Muslims. Only
if we die as Muslims, being conscious and fearful of Allah ﷻ, will we
be worthy of His mercy.

However some people feel that they can live they want in this life. Many
believe that they can live wild when they are young and repent to Allah
ﷻ when they get old; Of course Allah ﷻ can always forgive sins.
But we do not know the time of our death. It may come all of a sudden
without giving us a chance to repent. Many people die when they are
young even though most of us think it will only happen when we are old.
Allah's Mercy is for the *Muttaqūn*, who love Him, fear Him, and lead a
righteous life.

The situation of people who do not follow the right path and wait to repent right before death is described in the Qur'an:

$$\text{قَدْ خَسِرَ ٱلَّذِينَ كَذَّبُواْ بِلِقَآءِ ٱللَّهِ ۖ حَتَّىٰٓ إِذَا جَآءَتْهُمُ ٱلسَّاعَةُ بَغْتَةً قَالُواْ يَـٰحَسْرَتَنَا عَلَىٰ مَا فَرَّطْنَا فِيهَا وَهُمْ يَحْمِلُونَ أَوْزَارَهُمْ عَلَىٰ ظُهُورِهِمْ ۚ أَلَا سَآءَ مَا يَزِرُونَ}$$

"They indeed are the losers who deny their meeting with Allah, until the time when the hour (of death) comes upon them suddenly. They cry, 'Sadly for us that we ignored it!' They bear upon their back their burdens. Ah! Evil is the burden that they bare."
(al-'An'ām 6:31)

The *Muttaqūn* do not intentionally commit sins and then wait for their forgiveness. They avoid all evil acts and sinful activities altogether. In case they commit a mistake they immediately turn to Allah ﷻ in repentance and make a genuine *Tawbah*. When they die, the rewards of the *Jannah* await them.

Doing Good, Earning Good

A true believer is willing to sacrifice for his her beliefs. The Qur'an reminds us:

$$\text{لَن تَنَالُواْ ٱلْبِرَّ حَتَّىٰ تُنفِقُواْ مِمَّا تُحِبُّونَ}$$

You shall not reach good unless you
sacrifice what you love most.
('Āl 'Imrān 3:92)

A believer seeks his or her true reward from Allāh ﷻ

$$\text{إِنَّ ٱللَّهَ لَا يُضِيعُ أَجْرَ ٱلْمُحْسِنِينَ ﴿١٢٠﴾}$$

Indeed! Allāh does not waste the reward of those
who do good deeds.
(At-Tawbah 9:120)

WE HAVE LEARNED:

❖ The Believers must have *Taqwā*.

❖ The *Taqwā* means to fear and love Allāh ﷻ

❖ The Believers must live as true Muslims and die as true Muslims.

DO WE KNOW THESE WORDS?

Muttaqī

Muttaqūn

repent

steadfast

Taqwā

بِسْمِ اللّٰهِ الرَّحْمٰنِ الرَّحِيمِ

وَمِنَ ٱلنَّاسِ مَن يَقُولُ ءَامَنَّا بِٱللَّهِ وَبِٱلۡيَوۡمِ ٱلۡأَخِرِ وَمَا هُم بِمُؤۡمِنِينَ ﴿٨﴾

*Wa mina-(a)n-nāsi man yaqūlu 'āmanna bi-(A)llāhi
wa bi-(a)l-yawmi-a(a)l-'ākhiri wa-mā hum bi-Mu'minīn*

"And among the people are those who say, 'We believe in Allah and in the Last Day, but in fact, they are not of the believers.'"
(*Al-Baqarah* 2:8)

EXPLANATION:

Believing in Allah ﷻ and in the *'Ākhirah* is the core of Islamic faith. Without this belief, no one can honestly consider himself or herself a Muslim. However, saying that we believe in these things and then acting against them is, in fact, a form of disbelief. Saying one thing and acting against it is not true belief, but rather it is hypocrisy (*Nifāq*).

One who practices hypocrisy is called a hypocrite, or a *Munāfiq*. A *Munāfiq* is one who claims to act in a certain manner but in reality acts in a manner quite opposite to it. The *Munāfiqūn* (Hypocrites) are those people who claim to be Muslims, but in reality are disbelievers. When they are with the Muslims they say, "We are Believers." However, when they are with those opposed to Islam, they say, "We were only lying to the Muslims; we are actually on your side."

The *Munāfiqūn,* believe that they are successful in deceiving the Muslims in this way. However they are not deceiving anyone but themselves. Allah ﷻ is aware of what everyone really thinks and He is aware of how everyone really feels. Allah ﷻ knows how people act. He dislikes those people who say, "We believe," when they do not really believe.

Allah ﷻ knows who the true believers are and who are the *Munāfiqun* . During the time of Rasūlullāh ﷺ there was a group of people in Madīnah, who claimed that they honestly accepted Islam. They professed Islam to deceive the Muslims. As Muslims they attended the meetings of the believers. Then when they left, they passed on the secrets of the believers to the enemy.

During the conflict with the *Kuffār* of Makkah the *Munāfiqūn* played both sides. They participated in the _Shūrā_ meetings of the Muslims but spread deceitful ideas. They appeared to side with the believers, but at the last minute they would withdraw their support. When they were commanded to go out for battle, they made all kinds of excuses not to go. The _Munāfiqūn_ even established a _masjid_, called _Ad-Dirār,_ where they met secretly and conspired against the community. Rasūlullāh ﷺ was told through _Wahī_ the names of the _Munāfiqūn_ but he did not let the believers know. But many of the _Munāfiqūn_ were known to the Muslims because of their actions. Yet Rasūlullāh ﷺ did not want the believers to take revenge on the _Munāfiqūn._ He continued to tolerate them and treat them as Muslims.

During the last years of the life of Rasūlullāh ﷺ Allah ﷻ gave the _Munāfiqūn_ a chance to repent. He told Rasūlullāh ﷺ:

$$
يَٰٓأَيُّهَا ٱلنَّبِىُّ جَٰهِدِ ٱلْكُفَّارَ وَٱلْمُنَٰفِقِينَ وَٱغْلُظْ عَلَيْهِمْ وَمَأْوَىٰهُمْ جَهَنَّمُ وَبِئْسَ ٱلْمَصِيرُ ٧٣
$$

"O Prophet! Struggle against the Unbelievers and the _Munāfiqūn,_ and be firm against them. Their place is Hell--a horrible place indeed."
(_at-Tawbah_ 9:73)

Every community has always had its share of _Munāfiqūn_ from whom it must be protected. It is not always clear who a _Munāfiq_ really is. Like Rasūlullāh ﷺ we must be patient with all Muslims and continue to invite the community to follow the path of Islam. We must also be certain that our own faith and actions are truly Islamic. We must pray to Allah ﷻ for true faith and a united community.

WE HAVE LEARNED:

❖ _Munāfiqūn_ (Hyprocrites) are those people who claim to believe in Islam but, in fact they do not believe.

❖ _Nifāq_ (Hyprocrisy) is to say one thing but to act against it.

❖ The _Munāfiqūn_ do not deceive the Muslims but they only deceive themselves.

DO WE KNOW THESE WORDS?

deceive

hyprocrisy

hyprocrite

Masjid ad-Dirar

Munāfiq

Munāfiqūn

Nifāq

Lesson 13

The Best Community

بِسْمِ اللَّهِ الرَّحْمَٰنِ الرَّحِيمِ

كُنتُمْ خَيْرَ أُمَّةٍ أُخْرِجَتْ لِلنَّاسِ تَأْمُرُونَ بِالْمَعْرُوفِ
وَتَنْهَوْنَ عَنِ الْمُنكَرِ وَتُؤْمِنُونَ بِاللَّهِ

*Kuntum khaira 'ummatin 'ukhrijat li-(a)n-nāsi ta'murūna
bil-ma'rūfi wa-tanhawna 'an-(a)l-munkari wa-tu'minūna bi-
(A)llāhi*

"You are the best community which has been raised up among
humankind; you enjoin what is right and forbid what is wrong, and you
believe in Allah."
(*'Āl-'Imrān* 3:110)

EXPLANATION:

The best community is the one which serves Allah ﷻ and works to call
all of humanity to live righteously and avoid evil. The Muslim community
opens its arms to all people, rejecting the barriers of nationality, race,
language or culture. Because all humans are creations of Allah ﷻ, each
person is entitled to a position within the *'Ummah* of Muhammad ﷺ.

Being or becoming a member of this *'Ummah* depends on a person's
actions and beliefs. Even people who are born into Muslim families are not
automatically believers. If they do not act according to Allah's commands
and do not hold correct values they cannot truly have a place in this community.

The Qur'an says that there are three important reasons for Muslims to be
the best community:

❖ First, Muslims practice what is right and invite others to do
good.

❖ Second, sincere Muslims avoid what is sinful and help others
to avoid it too.

❖ Finally, they believe that Allah ﷻ is One, and His laws
and commands are to be obeyed.

As Muslims, we know that Allah's laws and teachings are the best for us. The Qur'an and the *Sunnah* are the two guides that tell us what is good and liked by Allah ﷻ and what is evil and disliked by Him.

The desire to do righteous things and to stop wrong things is what can make Muslims the very best community. However, we must remember that Muslims are not a race or nation or even a community like any other. Therefore, anyone who shares these righteous goals, believes in One God and in Prophet Muhammad ﷺ, acts like a true Muslim, is a welcomed member of the Muslim *'Ummah*.

WE HAVE LEARNED:

❖ The Muslims are the best of *'Ummah* raised by Allāh ﷻ

❖ We Muslims are not best of *'Ummah* because of our color, race or language.

❖ We are the best *'Ummah* because we enjoin what is right and forbid what is evil.

DO WE KNOW THESE WORDS?

enjoin

forbid

inferior

righteous

superior

Friendship of the Believers

بِسْمِ اللّٰهِ الرَّحْمٰنِ الرَّحِيمِ

وَالْمُؤْمِنُونَ وَالْمُؤْمِنَٰتُ بَعْضُهُمْ أَوْلِيَآءُ بَعْضٍ يَأْمُرُونَ بِالْمَعْرُوفِ وَيَنْهَوْنَ عَنِ الْمُنكَرِ وَيُقِيمُونَ الصَّلَوٰةَ وَيُؤْتُونَ الزَّكَوٰةَ وَيُطِيعُونَ اللّٰهَ وَرَسُولَهُ

*Wa-(a)l-Mu'minūna wa(a)l-Mu'minātu ba'du-hum 'awliyāu' ba'd(in),
ya' murūna bi-(a)l- ma'rūfi wa yanhawn 'ani-(a)l-munkari
wa yuqīmūna-(a)s-Salāta wa yu'tūna-(a)z-Zakāta
wa- yutī 'ūna-(A)llāha wa Rasūla-hu*

"The believing men and believing women are friends and protectors of one another; they enjoin the right and forbid the wrong and they establish the *Salāh* and they pay the *Zakāh*, and obey Allah and His Messenger."
(*at-Tawbah* 9:71)

EXPLANATION:

The believers are true friends and protectors of one another. Friends share many things with each other. They do many things together. They help one another through problems and protect each other from harm.

As friends, Muslims have many things in common. Muslims share their belief in Allah ﷾, His book, the Qur'an, and His prophet, Muhammad ﷺ. Muslims observe many acts of worship together every day. They pray, fast and perform *Hajj* together. They do many good deeds of charity together.

All Muslims have a common goal: to invite everyone to do right and help them to avoid doing wrong. Muslims perform those things that help society and forbid those things that divide society and destroy its peace. Muslims have the guidance of the Qur'an and the *Sunnah* and they share message contained within with everyone.

Common beliefs, common acts and common purposes make the Muslims one family and one *'Ummah*.

Rasūlullāh ﷺ described the Muslim 'Ummah in the most beautiful manner:

"You will see the believers, in their relationships to each other--based upon mercy love and kindness—as a single body; if one part of it gets sick the entire body is restless and in pain."
(Al-Bukhārī, Muslim)

Unity of Believers

Allāh ﷻ enjoins upon Muslims to remain united:

وَٱعۡتَصِمُواْ بِحَبۡلِ ٱللَّهِ جَمِيعٗا وَلَا تَفَرَّقُواْ

وَٱذۡكُرُواْ نِعۡمَتَ ٱللَّهِ عَلَيۡكُمۡ إِذۡ كُنتُمۡ أَعۡدَآءٗ فَأَلَّفَ بَيۡنَ قُلُوبِكُمۡ

فَأَصۡبَحۡتُم بِنِعۡمَتِهِۦٓ إِخۡوَٰنٗا وَكُنتُمۡ عَلَىٰ شَفَا حُفۡرَةٖ مِّنَ ٱلنَّارِ

فَأَنقَذَكُم مِّنۡهَاۗ كَذَٰلِكَ يُبَيِّنُ ٱللَّهُ لَكُمۡ ءَايَٰتِهِۦ لَعَلَّكُمۡ تَهۡتَدُونَ ﴿١٠٣﴾

And hold fast all together to the Rope of Allāh and be not divided among yourselves. And remember Allāh's favors on you: for you were enemies and He joined your hearts together in love, as that by His blessing you became brethren. And you were on the brink of the pit of Fire, and He saved you from it. Thus, does Allāh makes His signs clear to you that you may be guided.
('Āl 'Imrān 3:103)

WE HAVE LEARNED:

❖ All Believers are friends and support each other in doing good and forbidding evil.

❖ All Muslims share their beliefs and actions.

❖ The Muslims must remain united, help, and support each other in righteousness.

DO WE KNOW THESE WORDS?

protectors

relationship

righteousness

Rope of Allāh ﷻ

support

بِسْمِ اللهِ الرَّحْمَٰنِ الرَّحِيمِ

إِنَّمَا ٱلْمُؤْمِنُونَ إِخْوَةٌ فَأَصْلِحُوا بَيْنَ أَخَوَيْكُمْ ۚ
وَٱتَّقُوا ٱللَّهَ لَعَلَّكُمْ تُرْحَمُونَ ۝

'Innama (a)l-Mu'minūna 'ikhwatun,fa 'a slihū baina 'akhawai-kum,
wa-(a)t-taqu Allaha la'alla-kum turhamūn

"Indeed! The Believers are one brotherhood. So make peace
between your brothers, and fear Allah, that you may receive mercy."
(al-Hujurāt 49:10)

EXPLANATION:

All Muslims belong to one family. We are brothers and sisters to one
another. Just as we care for the members of our own families, we must
care for the people in the Islamic community. We want to see our family
united and working together for the benefit of every other family member.
Similarly, we want to see the Muslim *'Ummah* united and working
together for the cause of Allah ﷻ.

Islam is the religion of peace. Muslims are instructed by Allah ﷻ to
live in peace with everyone. Muslims must especially live in peace with
each other.

When a Muslim sees another Muslim, he greets him with *"As-
Salāmu 'Alaikum." As-Salāmu 'Alaikum* means "peace be with you." This
greeting is returned by saying *"Wa-'Alaikum As-Salām"* which means
"and upon you be peace too."

A Muslims always wishes well for another Muslim and never intentionally
does any harm to them. Real Muslims are full of mercy and caring for
each other. According to Rasūlullāh ﷺ, "A believer is a mirror of a
believer." *(al-Mishkāt)*

Whenever we see a Muslim brother or sister in need we should rush to
help him or her. If we find them doing wrong, we should gently correct
them. Preventing a Muslim from doing wrong is an act of friendship and
brotherhood.

Rasūlullāh ﷺ said, "Always help your brother, whether he is the
oppressor or the oppressed."

His *Sahabah* asked him, "O Rasūlullāh! We know how to help a person who is oppressed, but we do not know how to help if he is an oppressor."

Rasūlullāh ﷺ replied, "By stopping him from his act of oppression. This is your support for him" *(Al-Bukhārī, Muslim)*

A true Muslim always shares his or her blessings with relatives, friends, good causes and the poor. He or she gives *Zakāh* each year and *Sadaqah* whenever there is extra money. A true Muslim exchanges gifts with relatives and friends. He or she invites guests home and takes care of his or her neighbor's needs.

Two Muslims or two groups of Muslims may sometimes have differences among themselves. It is the duty of all believers to make peace. We should ask those who are fighting or arguing to fear Allah ﷻ and to follow the way of Islam. Allah's mercy and kindness are always with those who try to bring Muslims together.

Muslim unity is not only a blessing for the *'Ummah,* it is a blessing for everyone. The Muslim community strives to achieve peace and well-being for all of Allah's creations.

WE HAVE LEARNED:

❖ All Muslims are brothers and sisters to each other.

❖ Muslims must care for each other and support each other.

❖ If there is dispute or war between Muslims, we must work together to create peace and bring the warring Muslims together.

DO WE KNOW THESE WORDS?

brotherhood

differences

oppressed

oppressor

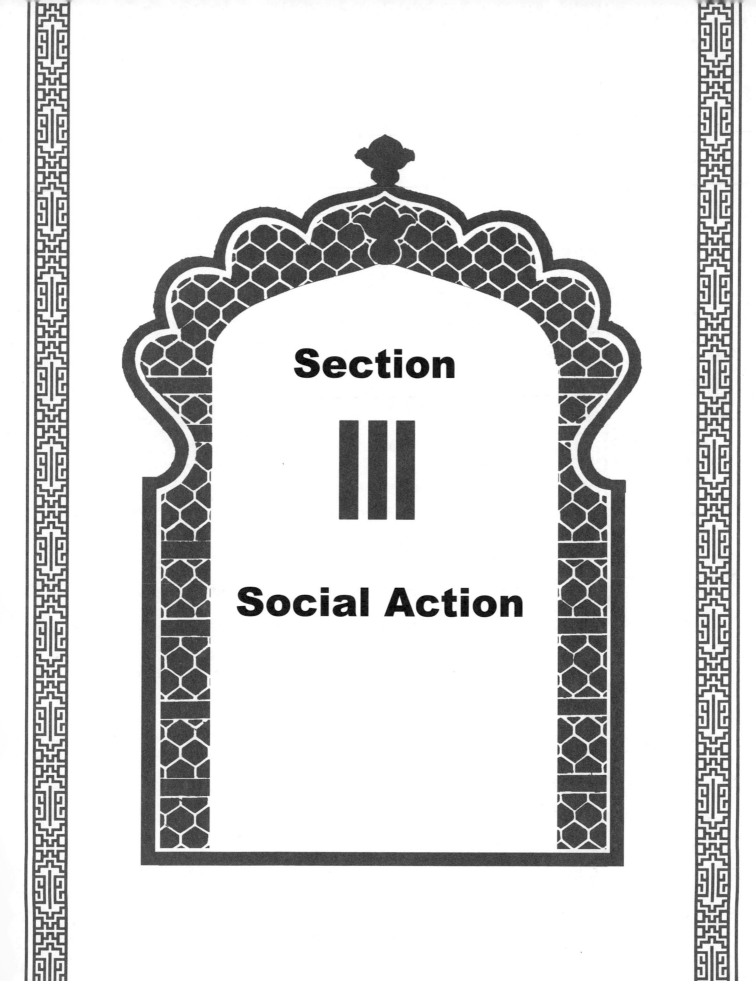

Section

III

Social Action

Doing the Right Thing

بِسْمِ اللهِ الرَّحْمٰنِ الرَّحِيمِ

مَنْ عَمِلَ صَٰلِحًا مِّن ذَكَرٍ أَوْ أُنثَىٰ
وَهُوَ مُؤْمِنٌ فَلَنُحْيِيَنَّهُۥ حَيَوٰةً طَيِّبَةً ۖ وَلَنَجْزِيَنَّهُمْ أَجْرَهُم
بِأَحْسَنِ مَا كَانُواْ يَعْمَلُونَ ﴿٩٧﴾

"Whoever does good deeds, whether male or female, and is
a believer, We will make them live a clean and pure life, and We will
give to such their reward according to the best of their actions."
(an-Nahl 16:97)

EXPLANATION:

It is one thing to have faith and another thing to live that faith
through everyday actions. How do we know what actions are right
in Islam? The Qur'an teaches us which beliefs and actions are right.
Rasūlullāh ﷺ has shown us how to follow the Qur'an, which is the
best model and example for us to follow. If we lead a life of faith and
right action, Allah ﷻ supports us and keeps us on the correct path.
He helps us to lead pure and clean lives.

Believers receive many rewards for leading righteous lives. They
receive the blessings of Allah ﷻ in this life. Leading a pure and
righteous life is a reward in itself. A person who has a clean heart
and a pure life does not have to fear anything. He or she leads a life
of peace and happiness. Allah ﷻ protects him or her and blesses
them with His mercy.

The blessings of Allah ﷻ take many shapes and forms. Allah ﷻ
blesses us with good parents, trusted friends and caring relatives.
Everyone in society respects an honest person and always comes to
his or her aid.

The true reward for believer is, in fact, in the 'Ākhirah. Such a person
will be warmly welcomed into Jannah, the gardens of 'Ākhirah.
Allah ﷻ will reward believers according to the best of their
intentions and actions.

The rewards of our good deeds cannot be measured in worldly
terms. Good deeds also bring many other rewards that we can't see

or count. Rasūlullāh ﷺ informed us of the effects of some of our good actions:

- Doing good deeds saves a person from a painful death;

- Charity in secrecy extinguishes the anger of Allah ﷻ;

- Generosity to relatives increases one's age.
(At-Targhib wa-(a)t-Tarhīb)

Islam wants us to have true belief and to be upright in all our actions. Allah ﷻ does not like those who say one thing then do another. The Qur'an always reminds us that the reward of Jannah is for those whose beliefs are supported by right actions:

إِنَّ ٱلَّذِينَ ءَامَنُواْ وَعَمِلُواْ ٱلصَّٰلِحَٰتِ كَانَتْ لَهُمْ جَنَّٰتُ ٱلْفِرْدَوْسِ نُزُلاً ۝

"Indeed! those who believe and do good deeds, theirs are the Gardens of Paradise for welcome."
(al-Kahf 18:107)

Doing Good and Evil

إِنْ أَحْسَنتُمْ أَحْسَنتُمْ لِأَنفُسِكُمْ وَإِنْ أَسَأْتُمْ فَلَهَا

If you do good, you do good yourself,
If you do evil(you do evil) against yourself.
(Al-'Isra' 17:7)

Compete for Good

بِسْمِ اللَّهِ الرَّحْمَٰنِ الرَّحِيمِ

وَلِكُلٍّ وِجْهَةٌ هُوَ مُوَلِّيهَا ۖ فَاسْتَبِقُوا الْخَيْرَاتِ ۚ أَيْنَ مَا تَكُونُوا يَأْتِ بِكُمُ اللَّهُ جَمِيعًا ۚ إِنَّ اللَّهَ عَلَىٰ كُلِّ شَيْءٍ قَدِيرٌ ﴿١٤٨﴾

"Each one has a goal to which he turns, so compete
with each other toward all that is good. And
wherever you are Allah will bring you all before Him.
Surely, Allah has power over all things."
(al-Baqarah 2:148)

EXPLANATION:

All of us have dreams and desires. We all want to achieve certain
goals in our lives. Here in this world we struggle to achieve all the
dreams that we hold dear. We often will do whatever it takes to attain
our goals. But as Muslims the main goal of life should be to please
Allah ﷻ. Everything we want to achieve must be in accordance to
the teachings of Islam.

In life, as in sports, we compete with each other to achieve our goals.
And as in sports there are rules that must be followed, boundaries
beyond which we cannot cross, and penalties for playing unfair. We
can succeed in our competition if we play by Allah's rules.

These rules are set by the Qur'an and the *Sunnah* and every
participant is a winner in this competition. When everyone in society
strives for the good of all, that society becomes better and better.
The rules of competition set by Allah ﷻ are not difficult, but easy.
When we follow Allah's Commands everyone benefits, Muslim and
non-Muslim alike. The true reward of this competition is gaining the
pleasure of *Jannah*.

The Qur'an promises:

سَابِقُوا إِلَىٰ مَغْفِرَةٍ مِّن رَّبِّكُمْ وَجَنَّةٍ عَرْضُهَا كَعَرْضِ السَّمَاءِ وَالْأَرْضِ أُعِدَّتْ لِلَّذِينَ آمَنُوا بِاللَّهِ وَرُسُلِهِ ۚ

"Therefore compete with one another for the forgiveness of your Lord, and for a Paradise as vast as Heaven and Earth prepared for those who believe in Allah and His Messengers."
(al-Hadīd 57:21)

Islam does not teach us to give up on the world to achieve the pleasures of *'Ākhirah*. Islam tells us to lead active and useful lives. The life of a believer is a constant *Jihād*, a struggle in the Name of Allah ﷻ. The results of our struggle and competition are in the hands of Allah ﷻ. As Muslims, we are taught to work for the best of this world and the best of the Hereafter.

True Competition

Once a man who was walking very fast, as if he was in a race, passed by Rasūlullāh ﷺ. A *Sahābī* saw the man and remarked, "How wonderful it would be if he were competing in this fashion in the way of Allah ﷻ." Rasūlullāh ﷺ heard his remark and said: "If this man is racing to earn a living for his children, it will be counted as being in the way of Allah ﷻ. If he is racing to support his elderly parents, it will still be regarded as being in the way of Allah ﷻ. Is he is racing for his own sake, to save himself from evil and mischief, it will still be considered as being in the way of Allah ﷻ. However, if he is racing to earn money to show off and impress others, it will be counted in the way of *Shāitān*."

(at-Targhīb wa-(a)t-Tarhīb)

WE HAVE LEARNED:

❖ A Muslim must struggle, strive and compete to achieve good.

❖ The Qur'ān and *Sunnah* teach us what is good and what is evil.

❖ A Muslim asks Allāh ﷻ for the best of this world and the best of the Hereafter.

DO WE KNOW THESE WORDS?

Bounty

compete

competitive

Jihad for Allāh

بِسْمِ اللّٰهِ الرَّحْمٰنِ الرَّحِيمِ

إِنَّمَا ٱلْمُؤْمِنُونَ ٱلَّذِينَ ءَامَنُوا بِٱللَّهِ وَرَسُولِهِ ثُمَّ لَمْ يَرْتَابُوا وَجَهَدُوا بِأَمْوَٰلِهِمْ وَأَنفُسِهِمْ فِى سَبِيلِ ٱللَّهِ ۚ أُوْلَـٰٓئِكَ هُمُ ٱلصَّـٰدِقُونَ ۝

'Inna-ma-(a)l-mu'minūna (a)lladhīna 'āmanū ni-(A)llāhi wa-
Rasūli-hi *thumma lam yartābū* wa –jāhadū bi- 'amwāli-him wa-
'anfusi-him fi sabīli-(A)llāhi, 'ulā'ika hum (a)s-sādiqūn

Those are true Believers, who have believed in Allāh and His
Messenger, and never since doubted, then made *Jihād*
(struggled) with their wealth and with their persons
in the Way of Allāh. Such are the sincere ones.
(Al-Hujurāt 49:15)

EXPLANATION:

Islām is a way of life which demands complete submission to Allāh
ﷻ There is a special action in Islām called *Jihād*, which means to
struggle and to strive in the Way of Allāh ﷻ To make *Jihād* in the
Way of Allāh ﷻ is one of the most important responsibilities in
Islām. The Qur'ān enjoins upon us:

وَجَهِدُوا فِى ٱللَّهِ حَقَّ جِهَادِهِ ۚ
هُوَ ٱجْتَبَىٰكُمْ وَمَا جَعَلَ عَلَيْكُمْ فِى ٱلدِّينِ مِنْ حَرَجٍ

And make the *Jihād* (struggle for the Sake of Allāh
as much as it must be made; He has chosen you and has made
no difficulties for you in religion…..
(Al-Hajj 22:78

The *Jihād* is made with one's money and with one's life. Spending
of wealth in the way of Allah ﷻ is *Jihād* made with money. Some
people have a great love of wealth and personal belongings. They
feel that wealth and possessions brings comfort and security to their
lives.

Islam teaches us that real comfort lies in remembering Allah ﷻ and
fulfilling our duties both to Him and to other human beings. There are
greater blessings and *Barakah* to be found in giving what we love most.

Jihād with one's life is to give one's time and to be prepared to suffer discomfort in the service of Islam. Then we serve others and support a good cause we may have to sacrifice our own security and comfort. Sometimes, we may have to suffer bodily harm.

Many times throughout history Muslims have been oppressed and forced to take up arms against their oppressors. Sometimes this was absolutely needed to defend one's self and to preserve Islam from those who wanted to kill Muslims. Fighting in the way of Allah ﷻ is also *Jihād*. Anyone who goes on this kind of *Jihād* knows that he may die and become a *Shahīd*, a martyr. A *Shahīd* goes straight to Paradise and lives there forever with Allah ﷻ. The purpose of *Jihād*, as in the purpose of life, is to seek the pleasure of Allah ﷻ.

However, we must remember that not every fight Muslims are involved in can be called *Jihād*. Simply fighting against non-Muslims does not make that fight a *Jihād*. One has to be very careful in taking sides on the basis of religion alone against non-Muslims. Islam believes in justice and respects the rights of everyone. Islam does not permit that injustice is done to any person, Muslim or non-Muslim.

Jihād as fighting has very special rules which must be strictly followed. It is also necessary to have a righteous *Amīr*, a leader, to command the Muslims on *Jihād*. Not everyone can simply start fighting and claim he or she is on *Jihād*. Sometimes people claim to be making *Jihād* but they do things that are not allowed in Islam. Allah ﷻ and His Messenger ﷺ have given us strict rules that the Muslims must follow for waging war. If a group claims to be making *Jihād* yet it fails to follow the rules of Islam how can it claim to be defending Islam?

Rasūlullāh ﷺ advised us that one of the greatest *Jihāds* is the one to control ourselves from immoral ideas and sinful actions. To control our anger and show patience in difficulties is a higher form of *Jihād*. This is called *Jihād an-Nafs* (*Nafs* means the self)

A Muslim should be able to participate in all forms of *Jihād* at all times. Allah ﷻ sends special help for those who make *Jihād* for Him:

WE HAVE LEARNED:

- ❖ *Jihād* means struggle and striving in the Path of Allāh ﷻ

- ❖ The Jihad as fighting has special rules and not every fight of a Muslim is a *Jihād*.

- ❖ Controlling one's anger and being patient in difficulties is a greater *Jihād*.

DO WE KNOW THESE WORDS?

Bounty

compete

competitive

Lesson 19

Shura: Mutual Consultation

بِسْمِ اللَّهِ الرَّحْمَنِ الرَّحِيمِ

وَأَمْرُهُمْ شُورَىٰ بَيْنَهُمْ

Wa-'amru-hum shūrā baina-hum….

And those who conduct their affairs by
consultation with each other….
(Ash- Shūrā 42:38)

EXPLANATION:

One of the best characteristics of the Muslim 'Ummah, as described
in the *ayat* above, is *Shūrā.* This is a word which means discussion,
consultation, and the asking of others' opinions on specific matters.

There is great *Barakah,* blessings, in asking other people's opinions.
Often, our own opinions on matters may not be fully informed.
Sometimes other people may have a better understanding of a matter
than we do. If someone offers us good advice, we should be ready to
listen and to follow.

In matters of religion we follow the Qur'an and the *Sunnah*; we do
not follow *Shūrā.* But there are many matters in our private lives or
community interests where the Qur'an and *Sunnah* do not give direct
guidance. In such matters it is advisable to seek *Shūrā.*

Rasūlullāh ﷺ was a messenger and he received revelations (*Wahī*)
from Allah ﷻ to guide him. In many worldly matters, however, he
asked the advice of his *Sahābah* and followed it. Allah ﷻ advised
him to consult his *Sahābah* and make decisions after consulting them:

وَشَاوِرْهُمْ فِي ٱلْأَمْرِ فَإِذَا عَزَمْتَ فَتَوَكَّلْ عَلَى ٱللَّهِ
إِنَّ ٱللَّهَ يُحِبُّ ٱلْمُتَوَكِّلِينَ ۝

"And consult them in (worldly) matters, when you have
taken a decision, put your trust in Allah, for Allah loves
those who put their trust in Him."
(Al 'Imran 3:159)

The *Khulafā' ar-Rāshidūn* and the *Sahābah* continued his practice of *Shūrā* in all worldly matters. In Islam there is no set method for *Shūrā*. *Shūrā* may take place at the individual level or in group meetings. The true spirit of *Shūrā* lies in openness to seek proper advice and the willingness to accept it.

During *Shūrā* we must discuss things with an open mind without getting angry or excited. We must listen to others carefully and respect their opinions. Any disagreements should not be taken personally but only as a difference of opinion. And when a final decision has been made, we must be ready to accept and follow it.

Shūrā is also valuable within one's family. Every family has its own problems and must solve them by mutual discussion; however, most family matters should not be discussed outside the home. These matters are best left within the family or with those whom the family trusts. In family issues we must show full respect to our elders and express our opinions in a courteous manner. In matters of common interest with friends and colleagues *Shūrā* can be very helpful. It is advisable to practice *Shūrā* within institutions, neighborhoods, and as nations.

Rasūlullāh ﷺ taught us that giving advice to someone is a form of trust. When someone asks us for advice, it is our duty to offer them the best advice possible. Sometimes we must give that advice in confidence. No one else, except the person seeking advice (*Shūrā*), should know anything about it.

Democracy is a form of *Shūrā*. A democratic government allows its citizens to participate in decision making. The opinions of the citizens influence the policies of the government and its decisions. In a democracy the opinions of the majority are always accepted.

When issues are put before *Shūrā*, we should find the best Islamic solution. Islamic *Shūrā* is more concerned with the well-being of all and its decisions are always in harmony with the teaching of Islam.

By opening ourselves to *Shūrā*, we declare the desire to solve our problems by mutual consultation while being conscious of Allah ﷻ and His Will for our lives.

WE HAVE LEARNED:

❖ The *Shūrā*, or mutual consultation, is an important aspect of Muslim life.

❖ Muslims must always follow the *Shūrā* except in matters of religion, where the Qur'an and Sunnah are clear.

❖ If Muslims live in a democratic society, they must participate in the proces, and try to influence its decision in favor of justice and truth.

DO WE KNOW THESE WORDS?

characteristic

consultation

democracy

process

Shūrā

بِسْمِ اللهِ الرَّحْمٰنِ الرَّحِيمِ

يَـٰٓأَيُّهَا ٱلَّذِينَ ءَامَنُوا لِمَ تَقُولُونَ مَا لَا تَفْعَلُونَ ﴿٢﴾ كَبُرَ مَقْتًا عِندَ ٱللَّهِ أَن تَقُولُوا مَا لَا تَفْعَلُونَ ﴿٣﴾

*Yā' ayyuha (a)lladhīna' āmanū lima taqūlūna mā lā taf' alūn(a).
Kabura maqtan 'ind(a)-Allāhi `an taqūlū mā lā-ta'falūna.*

Oh you who believe! Why do you say that which you do not do?
Most hateful it is in the Sight of Allāh, that you
say that which you do not do.
(As-Saff 61:2-3)

EXPLANATION:

A true Believer is one who believes in the Commandment of Allāh ﷻ and obeys them. His life is an example for other people. When he tells others to do something, he first does it himself.

Allāh ﷻ does not like those people who enjoin others to do good deeds but they themselves do not act upon them. Allāh ﷻ sent His Messenger ﷺ to set the best example of practice before preaching. Once *'Ummu(a)l-Mu'minin* 'Āishah ﵂ was asked about the *'Akhlāq* (the morals and manners) of Rasūlullāh ﷺ, she replied, "His *'Akhlāq* was the Qur'ān." Through his conduct, Rasūlullāh ﷺ showed to people how to practice the teachings of the Qur'ān. The life of Rasūlullāh ﷺ is the best example for us to follow. His life was the Qur'ān in practice. He was sent by Allāh ﷻ to show us how to follow the teaching of the Qur'ān in our life.

A true Believer acts according to his faith. A person who says one thing, but does another is called a *Munāfiq* in the Qur'ān. A Believer must always be known by his or her consistent practice of good acts. A Believer has the best *'Akhlāq*. He does not distinguish among the human beings on the basis of color, caste, race or religion. A Believer must be known not only by what he believes but what he practices.

The life of a Believer is a blessing wherever he lives. He or she joins hands with those who work for the good and fight against the mischief. He is always fair in his dealings. He avoids the company of evil people and prefers to be with the righteous. He respects

Practice What You Preach

his teachers, parents and elders and loves his youngsters. He makes his living only with *Halāl* means and avoids *Harām* means, even if he is going to benefit from them.

Allāh ﷻ knows the intentions of the people. He loves those who are sincere in their actions and do things to please Him. He does not like those people who teach something to others but they themselves do not practice it.

WE HAVE LEARNED:

❖ Allāh ﷻ hates those people who do not do themselves what they preach to others

❖ As Muslims we must always practice what we preach

❖ A Believer is known by his best *'Akhlāq* with everyone.

DO WE KNOW THESE WORDS?

Commandments

Munāfiq

preach

Be With The Truthful

بِسْمِ اللَّهِ الرَّحْمَٰنِ الرَّحِيمِ

يَـٰٓأَيُّهَا ٱلَّذِينَ ءَامَنُوا۟ ٱتَّقُوا۟ ٱللَّهَ
وَكُونُوا۟ مَعَ ٱلصَّـٰدِقِينَ ﴿١١٩﴾

Yā 'yyuha-(a)lladhīna 'āmanū-(a)t-taqu-(A)llāha
wa-kūnū ma'a-(a)s-sādiqīn(a)

Oh Believers, be careful of your duty to Allāh,
and be with the truthful people.
(At-Tawbah 9:119)

EXPLANATION:

We should always speak the truth and try to be in the company of the truthful. A person is judged by the company he or she keeps. The company of a Believer must consist of truthful, righteous and pious people.

Some people feel that if they are themselves good, then no one can influence them to do wrong. However, no matter how strong a person's faith may be, he or she will slowly be influenced by the people around him.

Having good and righteous friends who encourage us to live rightly is one of the best ways to ensure that we will not slip away from our faith and beliefs. On the other hand, we can be harmed by spending lots of time with people who disrespect our faith and disrespect what is accepted as right and wrong in society. We have a duty as Muslims to help all our friends to live righteous lives, avoiding what is dangerous and harmful.

When we are with our non-Muslim friends, we should not follow them in those things that are forbidden in Islām. We should explain to them what we, as Muslims, believe in and practice. However, we can work and cooperate with them in all things that are good and decent.

The best company we can find is our own family. We should send time with our parents, brothers and sisters, and other family members. We must also make Muslim friends, because they share our Islamic beliefs and they know what is *Halāl* and what is *Harām*. We must regularly visit the *Masjid* and attend Islamic schools. The best place in the Sight of Allāh 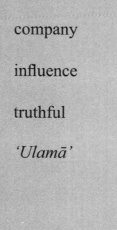 is a *Masjid*.

There are many good things that all religions preach and all human societies believe in. However, there are always those people who do not believe in any rules and disturb the peace of everyone. In societies where Muslims live with non-Muslims it is their responsibility to work together with other decent people to make society a better place for everyone. In modern society there are many freedoms. Some freedoms go against Islām. We must be especially careful in all those matters where Islam gives us clear guidance. Regular visits to our *Masjid*, membership and participation in Islamic Center work, spending our time with our family and Muslim friends can keep us on the Straight Path.

We should also study Islām in the company of other people at our Islamic Centers, at home, or in our neighborhoods. We must learn more about Islām from those who know and then teach it to others who want to know. We should sit with the *'Ulamā'* (people with Islamic knowledge) and our elders to learn about Islām and from their good example.

THE BEST COMPANY

'Abdullah 'ibn 'Abbās related that Rasūlullāh was asked, "whose company should we seek?"

Rasūlullāh replied, "The company of those whose seeing reminds you of Allāh, whose conversation increases your knowledge and whose actions inspire you to prepare for the *'Ākhirah*."
(At-Targhīb wa-(a)t-Tarhīb)

WE HAVE LEARNED:

❖ Good company will make us good and bad company will make us bad people.

❖ Allāh wants Muslims to be good and be in company of good people.

❖ We should work together with our non-Muslim friends in doing good things that are permitted in Islam

DO WE KNOW THESE WORDS?

company

influence

truthful

'Ulamā'

Lesson 22

Relations With The People of the Book

بِسْمِ اللَّهِ الرَّحْمَٰنِ الرَّحِيمِ

قُلْ يَٰأَهْلَ ٱلْكِتَٰبِ تَعَالَوْا۟ إِلَىٰ كَلِمَةٍ سَوَآءٍ بَيْنَنَا وَبَيْنَكُمْ أَلَّا نَعْبُدَ إِلَّا ٱللَّهَ وَلَا نُشْرِكَ بِهِۦ شَيْـًٔا وَلَا يَتَّخِذَ بَعْضُنَا بَعْضًا أَرْبَابًا مِّن دُونِ ٱللَّهِ فَإِن تَوَلَّوْا۟ فَقُولُوا۟ ٱشْهَدُوا۟ بِأَنَّا مُسْلِمُونَ ۝

*Qul yā 'ahl-al-kitābi ta'alaw 'ilā kalimatin sawā' in baina-na
wa baina-kum 'anlā-ta'budū 'illā (A)llāhā wa-la nushrika bi-hī
shai' an wa-lā yattakhidha ba'duna
ba'dan 'arbāban min dūni-(A)llāhi fa-'in tawallaw fā-qūlu (a)-
shhadū bi-'annā Muslimūna*

O People of the Book, come to common terms as between us and
you: that we worship none except Allāh; that we associate no
partners with Him, and that none of us shall take others from
among ourselves as Lords and Patrons other than Allāh.
And if they turn away say, "Bear witness that we are Muslims
(submitting to Allāh's Commands)"
('Āl 'Imrān 3:64)

EXPLANATION:

We Muslims believe that Islām is the original religion of humanity.
It is also the Final Message of Allāh ﷻ Although every people in
the world has received this message, much of the message was lost
over time. Its pure and original teachings got mixed up with many
teaching of *Shirk* and *Kufr.*

Some of the earlier people who received the Divine Revelations in
the form of Holy Books maintained the basic message, but they lost
many important details. Rasūlullāh ﷺ was sent as the messenger
with the Final Message the Qur'ān. The Qur'ān not only corrects
the wrong beliefs that developed in the earlier religions, but it also
completes the teaching of earlier prophets.

Three groups who received earlier Divine Books are specifically
recognized in the Qur'ān as the "People of the Book". These three

groups are the Jews, the Christians and the Sabeans. The Jews and the Christians exist until now, while the Sabeans have disappeared as their followers accepted one of the other major religions.

The Muslims have a special relationship with the entire human religious family, but with the Jews and the Christians they have very special relations. The fact that Allāh ﷻ chose, both Jews and the Christians to receive His important Revelations (the *Tawrāt* and *Injīl*), entitles them to our special respect. I most matters, the Muslims have shown to other religious communities the same respect as that shown to the People of the Book.

The Qur'ān invites the People of the Book to unite with Muslins to work for righteousness on the basis of their common belief in the One God. However, if they reject the offer of the Muslims, the Muslims are require to continue to work for the good of everyone.

There is no doubt that Islām is the only accepted religion with Allāh ﷻ, but Islām recognizes the rights of other people to believe and practice to work together for common good:

$$\text{وَتَعَاوَنُواْ عَلَى ٱلْبِرِّ وَٱلتَّقْوَىٰ}$$

$$\text{وَلَا تَعَاوَنُواْ عَلَى ٱلْإِثْمِ وَٱلْعُدْوَٰنِ}$$

And help each other in goodness and piety and
do not cooperate with one another in sin and aggression.
(*Al-Mā'idah 5:2*)

بِسْمِ اللهِ الرَّحْمَنِ الرَّحِيمِ

وَلَا تُجَـٰدِلُوٓا۟ أَهْلَ ٱلْكِتَـٰبِ إِلَّا بِٱلَّتِى هِىَ أَحْسَنُ إِلَّا ٱلَّذِينَ ظَلَمُوا۟ مِنْهُمْ ۖ وَقُولُوٓا۟ ءَامَنَّا بِٱلَّذِىٓ أُنزِلَ إِلَيْنَا وَأُنزِلَ إِلَيْكُمْ وَإِلَـٰهُنَا وَإِلَـٰهُكُمْ وَٰحِدٌ وَنَحْنُ لَهُۥ مُسْلِمُونَ ۝

*Wa-lā tujādilū' Ahla (a)l-Kitābi 'illā bi-(a)llatī hiya 'ahsan(u),
'illā (a)lladhīna zalamū min-hum, wa qūlū 'amannā bi-(a)lladhī
'unzila 'ilai-nā wa unzila 'ilai-kum wa Illāhu-nā wa Ilāhu-kum
Wāhidun wa- nahnu la-hū Muslimūn.*

"And do not argue with the People of the Book except in a
beautiful manner, unless it be with those who do wrong (to
Muslims): And say to them "We believe in the Revelation that
came down to us and in that which came down to you; Our God and
your God is One; and it is to Him that we submit in Islām."
(Al-'Ankabūt 29:46)

EXPLANATION:

Islām accepts that the world is pluralistic. "Pluralistic" means that
there are many kinds of people in the world and all of them have the
same rights as human beings. The differences of colors, languages,
tribes, and nations are created by Allāh ﷻ No one must claim
superiority for these reasons.

There are many religions in the world. Allāh ﷻ sent his messengers
to all people with the same message of Islām. Every faith group
believes that their message is better than any other. Some religions
like Hinduism, Judaism, Zoroastrianism do not believe in converting
others to their religion. Others like Christianity, Islam, and Buddhism
believe in inviting others to their religion.

When people live together, it is natural to discuss issues of religion
and other matters with each other. Those people who are friends,
neighbors, and colleagues must work together and discuss with each
other in a gentle and respectful manner. The purpose of discussion
is to have a dialogue and not to insult and abuse. Muslims are asked
to talk to the People of the Book (in fact, all religious humankind)
kindly.

However, if the Muslims are oppressed, then they are not required to
follow the same etiquette. Oppression is worse than killing, and an

oppressed person is allowed to react in many ways than would be otherwise unacceptable.

Muslims must also emphasize that their God and the God of the People of the Book is the same. Thus the People of the Book and the Muslims have a solid base upon which to build a lasting peaceful friendship.

There are many kinds of religions in the world. There are still some people who worship idols, trees, rivers and other natural objects. We have to speak kindly to them also, and explain the message of *Tawhīd*. Islām forbids us to revile the idols, images, and gods or to make fun of their beliefs:

لَيْسُوا۟ سَوَآءً ۗ مِّنْ أَهْلِ ٱلْكِتَٰبِ أُمَّةٌ قَآئِمَةٌ
يَتْلُونَ ءَايَٰتِ ٱللَّهِ ءَانَآءَ ٱلَّيْلِ وَهُمْ يَسْجُدُونَ ۝ يُؤْمِنُونَ
بِٱللَّهِ وَٱلْيَوْمِ ٱلْءَاخِرِ وَيَأْمُرُونَ بِٱلْمَعْرُوفِ وَيَنْهَوْنَ عَنِ ٱلْمُنكَرِ
وَيُسَٰرِعُونَ فِى ٱلْخَيْرَٰتِ وَأُو۟لَٰٓئِكَ مِنَ ٱلصَّٰلِحِينَ ۝

Not all of them (the People of the Book) are alike: there is a community that stands (for truth); they recite the Signs of Allāh all night long, and the prostrate before Him.
They believe in Allāh and the Last Day; they enjoin what is right, and forbid what is wrong; and they hasten to do good works; they are of the righteous.
(*'Āl 'Imrān 3:113-114*)

Many of the People of the Book, during the time of Rasūlullāh ﷺ and ever since, have accepted Islām and became part of the 'Ummah of Rasūlullāh ﷺ As Islām spread into various parts of the world, people of many faiths joined it. Most of the Muslim lands of the Middle East today were once Christian.

When Islām spread to non-Christian areas (Iran, India, Central Asia, the Far East, etc.), Muslim rulers treated all other inhabitants with the same respect as the People of the Book. Not only the Jews and the Christians but all the minorities in the Muslim lands enjoyed religious freedom.

Since Muslims live in a world in which people follow different faith, Allāh ﷻ wants them to live in peace with others. Allāh ﷻ wants Muslims to cooperate with others in doing what is right and to avoid and wrong-doing. Leading a good Islamic life is the best form of *Da'wah*.

WE HAVE LEARNED:

❖ Islām gives special respect to the People of the Book.

❖ We must respect other peoples' faiths, make and leave their guidance to Allāh ﷻ

DO WE KNOW THESE WORDS?

conversion

dialogue

Islamic life

oppression

pluralistic

Zoroastrianism

Verify the News

بِسْمِ اللهِ الرَّحْمَنِ الرَّحِيمِ

يَـٰٓأَيُّهَا ٱلَّذِينَ ءَامَنُوٓا۟ إِن جَآءَكُمْ فَاسِقٌۢ بِنَبَإٍ فَتَبَيَّنُوٓا۟
أَن تُصِيبُوا۟ قَوْمًۢا بِجَهَـٰلَةٍ فَتُصْبِحُوا۟ عَلَىٰ مَا فَعَلْتُمْ نَـٰدِمِينَ ۝

*Yā'ayyuha-(a)lladhīna 'āmanū 'in jā'a-kum fāsiqun bi-naba' in fa-
tabayyanū 'an tusībū qawman bi- jahālatin fa-tusbihū 'alā mā
fa'altum nādimin(a)*

O you who believe! If an evil person brings you news, verify
its truth, in case you harm people unknowingly, and later
feel sorry for what you have done.
(Al-Hujurāt 49:6)

EXPLANATION:

People generally believe whatever they are told. Everyday, we hear
things that are good or bad, true or false. Sometimes, the things that
are being said deal with other people and sometimes they deal with
us directly. If we want to take action on some matter based upon the
information we receive, we must verify the news first.

Often, when we hear something, we do not hear it first hand.
Sometimes people deliberately say things out of mischief to mislead
us about a matter. Especially if a piece of news does not favor us or
cause us anger and anxiety we must verify it.

In order to verify any news, Allāh ﷻ tells the Believers to find
out the nature of the person relating the news. We must find out if
his intentions are good or bad, and we must find out his reasons for
relating the news to us.

In every society there are evil people who go around backbiting and
spreading rumors. Often, they find ready listeners among ignorant
and idle people. Sometimes, we ourselves start enjoying the gossip.
We may even make a mistake and pass this gossip to others as news.

A simple story often gets mixed up and misreported. It may hurt many
people and create hostile feelings. Many times the victims of the
gossip do not even know the reasons behind peoples' anger against
them. Many innocent people can suffer due to the evil behavior of a
few. What may start as a little joke can turn into serious trouble.

Although evil people do things for cruel fun or to harm others, most people do not like to hurt or harm anyone. They become innocent victims of false news of the evil-doer. If they get ever-excited they may do something in a fit of anger that they will later regret.

We must always try to verify any news we hear. Avoiding gossip and misinformation and keeping our distances from evil people are the wisest courses of action.

SPREADING RUMORS

'Abdullah ibn Mas'ūd related that Rasūlullāh ﷺ advised us:

"The *Shaitān* often takes the appearance of a human being and comes to the people disperse someone from among them says, 'I have heard such and such story. I remember his face but I don't know his name."

WE HAVE LEARNED:

❖ Whenever we hear something, we must always verify it.

❖ We should not act hastily, out of anger.

❖ We must not say or do things that we may later regret.

DO WE KNOW THESE WORDS?

embarrassed

information

intention

verify

Builders of Masajid

بِسْمِ اللَّهِ الرَّحْمَنِ الرَّحِيمِ

إِنَّمَا يَعْمُرُ مَسَاجِدَ اللَّهِ مَنْ ءَامَنَ بِاللَّهِ وَالْيَوْمِ الْأَخِرِ وَأَقَامَ الصَّلَوٰةَ وَءَاتَى الزَّكَوٰةَ وَلَمْ يَخْشَ إِلَّا اللَّهَ

'Innamā ya'murū masājid-Allāhi man 'āmana bi-(A)llāhi wa (a)l-yawmi (a)l-'Ākhiri wa-'aqāma (a)s-Salāta wa-'ātu az-Zakāta wa-lam yakhsha illa (A)llāha...

He indeed shall build and maintain the mosque for Allāh, who believes in Allāh and the Last Day, offers regular prayer, and gives the *Zakāh* and fears none except Allāh
(At-Tawbah 9:18)

EXPLANATION:

A *Masjid* is a very important institution in Islām. One of the duties of a true Believer is that he builds, maintains and visits the *Masjid* regularly.

Allāh ﷻ chooses very special people to build *Masājid* for Him. Allāh ﷻ wants only the Believers to build *Masājid* for Him; He does not want the *Kuffār* to build *Masājid* for Him.

A *Masjid* is a place where Muslims gather for regular prayer and for other religious and social activities. Allāh ﷻ asked 'Ibrāhīm ﷺ and his son 'Ismā'īl ﷺ to build the Ka'bah as *Bait- Allāh* (the House of Allāh), for people to come together from all over the world to worship Him. *Bait Allāh* is the first *Masjid* ever built.

Allāh ﷻ asked 'Ibrāhīm ﷺ to invite people to perform the *Hajj* (Pilgrimage) in the House of Allāh ﷻ

After some time, the Makkans forgot the teachings of their prophets and made the *Ka'bah a house of idols. Rasūlullāh ﷺ once again made the* Ka'bah the House of Allāh ﷻ When Rasūlullāh ﷺ went to Madīnah, he stopped at Qubā' and built the first *Masjid* of Madīnah. Those who go to Qubā' with the intention to offer two *Raf'ah* of *Na* receive the *thawāb* (reward) of one *'Umrah.*

As soon as Rasūlullāh ﷺ settled down in Madīnah, he purchased a plot of land and build the *Masjid an-Nabī*. The first *Masjid an-Nabī* was built by Rasūlullāh ﷺ and his *Sahābah*. It has since been extended many times.

When the Muslims liberated Jerusalem, 'Umar ؓ built a *Masjid* at the Rock, the location where Rasūlullāh ﷺ went for his journey into the Heavens. The *Masjid* was built at the site where Prophet Sulaimān ؑ had built his *Masjid* and it is called *Bait al-Maqdas,* the Sacred House. *Bait-Allāh, Masjid an-Nabī* and *Bait al-Maqdas* are the three most important *masājid* of Islām and must be visited, if one can afford it.

Muslims have built many *masājid* all across the world as the number of Muslims grew steadily. These *masājid* are the centers of Islamic life. It is the duty of every muslim to visit his or her *masjid*, support it, and participate in building it.

Rasūlullāh ﷺ said:

> Those who build *Masājid*, maintain them and visit them regularly are the friends and beloved of Allāh.
> *(At-Tabarānī)*

Rasūlullāh ﷺ said:

"Whoever builds a *masjid* in this world, Allāh ﷻ builds a house for him in *Jannah*."
(Hadīth)

بِسْمِ اللهِ الرَّحْمٰنِ الرَّحِيمِ

وَمَا كَانَ ٱلْمُؤْمِنُونَ لِيَنفِرُواْ كَآفَّةً فَلَوْلَا نَفَرَ مِن كُلِّ فِرْقَةٍ مِّنْهُمْ طَآئِفَةٌ لِّيَتَفَقَّهُواْ فِى ٱلدِّينِ وَلِيُنذِرُواْ قَوْمَهُمْ إِذَا رَجَعُوٓاْ إِلَيْهِمْ لَعَلَّهُمْ يَحْذَرُونَ ﴿١٢٢﴾

Wa- mā kāna(a)l-Mu'minūna li-yanfirū kāffatan, fa-lawlā nafara min kulli firqatin min-hum tā' ifatun li-yatafaqqahū fid-dīni wa- li-yundhirū qawma-hum 'idha raja'ū' ilai-him la'alla-hum yahdharūn(a)

And the Believers should not all go forth (to make *Jihād*), of every troop only a group should remain behind; they should devote themselves to the studies of religion and that they may teach their people when they return, so that they may learn (to follow the Laws of Allāh).
(At-Tawbah 9:122)

EXPLANATION:

Seeking knowledge is very important in Islām. The first Revelation to Rasūlullāh ﷺ started with the word *Iqra'*, which means "read" or "proclaim." Allāh ﷻ sent Rasūlullāh ﷺ as a teacher to educate us about true faith and to guide us towards leading a moral life. Allāh ﷻ sent His Message through a Book of Guidance, the Qur'ān. A Muslim must strive hard to seek knowledge.

Rasūlullāh ﷺ said, "Seek knowledge is an obligation for every Muslim man and woman." *(Al-Baihaqī, Shu'ab al-'Imān)*

He also said, "Seek knowledge from the cradle to the grave."

"The best among you," said Rasūlullāh ﷺ, "are those who learn the Qur'ān and then teach it to others." *(Al-Bukhārī)*

The best knowledge is the knowledge of the Qur'ān and the *Sunnah* of Rasūlullāh ﷺ. It is through the Qur'ān and the *Sunnah* that we understand Islām and our duties as Muslims. As Muslims, we are required to seek and teach the knowledge which benefits others. We should not seek or teach the knowledge which harms others or is forbidden by Allāh ﷻ, Examples of evil knowledge are black magic, gambling, making liquor or drugs, practicing usury etc. Rasūlullāh ﷺ taught his followers a *Du'ā'* which says:

> "Oh Allāh, grant me beneficial knowledge and save me from harmful knowledge."
> *(Musnad 'Ahmad)*

While seeking knowledge is an obligation for every Muslim, Allāh ﷻ wants some of us to completely devote ourselves to the knowledge of our Dīn, Islām. For this group of people, seeking, studying and teaching Islamic knowledge is the most important duty they have, even more than physically fighting in the Name of Allāh ﷻ

Allāh ﷻ has given ranks to those who have knowledge:

يَرۡفَعِ ٱللَّهُ ٱلَّذِينَ ءَامَنُواْ مِنكُمۡ وَٱلَّذِينَ أُوتُواْ ٱلۡعِلۡمَ دَرَجَٰتٍۚ وَٱللَّهُ بِمَا تَعۡمَلُونَ خَبِيرٌ ۝

Allāh will exalt those who believe among you, and those who have knowledge, to higher ranks, Allāh is informed of what you do.
(Al-Mujādilah 58:11)

The Qur'ān further says:

قُلۡ هَلۡ يَسۡتَوِى ٱلَّذِينَ يَعۡلَمُونَ وَٱلَّذِينَ لَا يَعۡلَمُونَۗ إِنَّمَا يَتَذَكَّرُ أُوْلُواْ ٱلۡأَلۡبَٰبِ ۝

Are those who know equal to those who do not Know? But only people of understanding will pay heed.
(Az-Zumār 39:9)

WE HAVE LEARNED:

❖ Seeking knowledge is an obligation for every Muslim man and woman.

❖ A group of Muslims must dedicate themselves to learning and teaching.

❖ Those who have knowledge have greater rank than those who have no knowledge.

DO WE KNOW THESE WORDS?

dedicate

Beneficial knowledge

physical

rank

بِسْمِ ٱللَّهِ ٱلرَّحْمَٰنِ ٱلرَّحِيمِ

وَٱبْتَغِ فِيمَآ ءَاتَىٰكَ ٱللَّهُ ٱلدَّارَ ٱلْأَخِرَةَ ۖ وَلَا تَنسَ نَصِيبَكَ مِنَ ٱلدُّنْيَا ۖ وَأَحْسِن كَمَآ أَحْسَنَ ٱللَّهُ إِلَيْكَ ۖ وَلَا تَبْغِ ٱلْفَسَادَ فِى ٱلْأَرْضِ ۖ إِنَّ ٱللَّهَ لَا يُحِبُّ ٱلْمُفْسِدِينَ ۝

Wa-btaghi fi-mā 'āta-ka-(A)llāhu (a)d-Dā r-(a)l-'Ākhirata wa-lā tansā naṣība-ka mina (a)d-dunyā. Wa-'ahsin kamā 'ahsana-(A)llāhu 'ilai-ka, wa- lā tabghi-(a)l-fasāda fi (a)l-'ardi, 'Inn a-(A)llāha lā yuhibbu (a)l-mufsidīn.

And seek, with the (wealth) Allah has given you the home of the Hereafter, nor forget your share in this world; and be you kind as Allah has been kind to you. And seek not mischief in the land: for Allah loves not those who make mischief.

(Al-Qasas 28:77)

EXPLANATION:

The real home of the true Believers is the *'Ākhirah*, but they have a share in this world too. According to Rasulullāh ﷺ, this world is "the crop of the *'Ākhirah*." Whatever we plant in this world, we shall harvest in the *'Ākhirah*.

All actions of true Muslims are done to please Allāh ﷻ and to seek reward in the *'Ākhirah*. This world has been created by Allāh ﷻ and as Muslims, we must work to make it a better place for all. We must use our power, positions and wealth for the Cause of Allāh ﷻ

If the Muslims do not take part in matters of this world, everyone will suffer. Even though so much of the word is so far from Islām, Allāh ﷻ does not want us to withdraw from or refuse to take part in this world. We cannot become closer to Allāh ﷻ by giving up of what He has created for us. Islām teaches us that we serve Allāh ﷻ best by serving our fellow human beings.

There are two kinds of rights in Islām: *Huqūq Allāh* (The Rights of Allāh) and *Huqūq al-'Ibād* (human rights). Both are important and as Muslims we must fulfill the rights of both.

As Muslims, we worship Allāh ﷻ alone and ask His help. In this world we live with fellow human beings, care for them and work with them to make our society a better place for all.

As Muslims, we must work to establish peace and justice on earth. This may only happen if everyone does good work and avoids evil. We must know that Allāh's Kindness is always with us and we should thank Him by being kind to others.

As responsible members of our society, we must all cooperate together. Whatever wealth, power, position or influence that Allāh ﷻ has blessed us with must be used for the benefit of everyone. If we do not become involved in the affairs of this world we cannot fulfill our Islamic duties.

WE HAVE LEARNED:

❖ A Muslim must not forget his share in this world.

❖ Islām does not allow a Muslim to withdraw from this world.

❖ A Muslim must use his share of this world to fulfill both *Huqūq Allāh* and *Huqūq al-ʻIbād*

DO WE KNOW THESE WORDS?

fulfill

Huqūq Allāh

Huqūq al-ʻIbād

Lesson

28

Remembrance

بِسْمِ اللَّهِ الرَّحْمَٰنِ الرَّحِيمِ

وَذَكِّرْ فَإِنَّ ٱلذِّكْرَىٰ تَنفَعُ ٱلْمُؤْمِنِينَ ۝

Wa-dhakkir fa 'inna-(a)dh-dhikrā tanfa'u-(a)l-Mu'minīn

(Oh Muhammad) go on reminding, for reminding benefits the
Believers.
(*Adh-Dhariyāt 51:55*)

EXPLANATION:

Rasūlullāh ﷺ was asked by Allāh ﷻ to remind the people to
remember Him, His religion Islām and their final home, Al-'Ākhirah.
Human beings are often forgetful. They forget about Allāh ﷻ and
the teachings of His Messengers.

The world has many pleasures and distractions that pull people away
from Allāh ﷻ. People become too busy and think only of his world,
and they forget Allāh's Commands and their duty towards Him.
Allāh ﷻ sent many messengers to remind human beings of their
duty to Allāh ﷻ. He revealed many books through the messengers
to remind people of His religion Islām.

However, people would soon forget the teachings of the prophets.
They would also forget the teachings of the books. The loved the
world and its pleasure so much that they changed the teachings of the
prophets to suit their ideas.

Rasūlullāh ﷺ was sent as the last Messenger and He received Allāh's
Last Book the Qur'ān. The message of the Qur'ān is a permanent
reminder to the Muslims to always remember Allāh's religion and
work for the 'Ākhirah.

Another name of the Qur'ān is the Tadhkīrah, the Reminder:

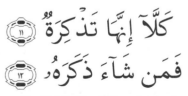

كَلَّا إِنَّهَا تَذْكِرَةٌ ۝

فَمَن شَاءَ ذَكَرَهُ ۝

Indeed this Qur'ān is a *Tadhkīrah*, (Reminder). So whoever wishes
can learn from it.
(*'Abasa 80:11-12*)

The Book of Allāh ﷻ and the *Sunnah* of Rasūlullāh ﷺ are the permanent reminders to humanity for all time to come. It is the duty of the Muslims to remind each other and all of humanity about the message of Islām.

A reminder is needed both for those who do not pay attention to the call of Allāh ﷻ and for those who have received the message and may not be giving it due attention. Even those who are conscious of their duty to Allāh ﷻ benefit from occasional reminders. All of us need to be reminded of our duty to remember Allāh ﷻ every once in a while.

Going to the *Masjid* is a strong reminder. In the *Masjid*, we think only of Allāh ﷻ. Being in the company of fellow Muslims is also a good reminder. Meeting the *'Ulamā'* and hearing their wise words is also a reminder. Reading the Qur'ān, studying the *Sīrah*, offering charity, and participating in good deeds all serve as reminders that we continue to remember Allāh ﷻ and His many Favors. Allāh ﷻ makes the most beautiful promise to those who remember Him:

$$\text{فَٱذْكُرُونِىٓ أَذْكُرْكُمْ وَٱشْكُرُواْ لِى وَلَا تَكْفُرُونِ ۱۵۲}$$

"So, remember Me and I will remember you. Give thanks to Me and do not deny My Favors."
(Al-Baqarah 2:152)

RECOMMENDING GOOD AND EVIL

مَّن يَشْفَعْ شَفَـٰعَةً حَسَنَةً يَكُن لَّهُۥ نَصِيبٌ مِّنْهَا

وَمَن يَشْفَعْ شَفَـٰعَةً سَيِّئَةً يَكُن لَّهُۥ كِفْلٌ مِّنْهَا

Whoever recommends and helps a good cause will have a share in its rewards, and whoever recommends and helps an evil cause, will share in its burden.
(An-Nisā 4:85)

فَمَن يَعْمَلْ مِثْقَالَ ذَرَّةٍ خَيْرًا يَرَهُۥ ۷

وَمَن يَعْمَلْ مِثْقَالَ ذَرَّةٍ شَرًّا يَرَهُۥ ۸

Then, anyone who has done an atom's weight of good, shall see it. And then anyone who has done an atom's weight of evil, shall see it.

WE HAVE LEARNED:

❖ Rasūlullāh ﷺ was asked by Allāh ﷻ to remind the Believers that they remember Him and His Mesasage

❖ Islām does not allow a Muslim to withdraw from this world.

❖ A Muslim must use his share of this world to fulfill both *Huqūq Allāh* and *Huqūq al-'Ibād*

DO WE KNOW THESE WORDS?

consult

reminding

natural

بِسْمِ اللَّهِ الرَّحْمَنِ الرَّحِيمِ

A

'Adl: justice

'Ashraf al-Makhluqat: literally: the most honorable of creations. Term referring to the human being as the best of Allāh's creations.

atom's weight: very very small weight

B

Bait-Allāh: literally: the House of Allāh. The Ka'bah; or any mosque.

Bait al-Maqdis: Jerusalem (Quds) mosque; the first Qibla.

bearer of burdens: (n) everyone is responsible for his/her actions.

beliefs: (n) convictions, certainties, faith.

bounty: (n) an abundance of something, a charity.

Brotherhood: (n) feelings of connection and kinship.

C

careless: (a) inattentive, thoughtless.

caste system: (n) The Hindu system of distinct and hereditary social classes, each of which is prohibited from dealings with the other.

characteristic: (n) aspects, qualities.

commandments: (n) orders, set rules.

common good: (n) something which benefits everyone involved.

company: (n) a gathering; those with whom one associates; a business or organization.

compel: (v) to force someone to do something.

compensation: (n) a payment for services rendered.

compete: (v) to contend, to rival someone for something as in a race or contest.

competitive: (a) one who seeks and thrives on competition.

consult: (v) to seek counselor advice regarding some matter.

consultation: (n) the counseling received.

constitution: (n) a code of laws; a charter.

conversion: (n) change, transformation. Ex: to convert from Christianity to Islām.

cooperate: (v) to participate with someone else for a common goal.

criminals: (n) anyone who willingly breaks the law.
crucify: (v) to execute by nailing to a cross.

D

Da'wah: (n) literally: a Call. Da'wah involves calling people to Islām. Evangelism.
deceive: (v) to lie; to willingly mislead someone.
dedicate: (v) to commit; to pledge; to devote.
democracy: (n) a representative form of government. The citizens of a democracy express their views and needs by electing who will speak for them (represent them) in the legislature (the branch of government which makes laws).
differences: (n) variation; contrast; distinction; argument.

E

embarrassed: (adj) a state of humiliation or extreme shame and discomfort.
emotions: (n) feelings such as anger, sadness, happiness, etc.
encourage: (v) to inspire, to cheer along.
enjoin: (v) to command, to urge, to warn.

F

faith: (n) belief, trust, confidence.
forbid: (v) to prohibit, to outlaw.
fulfill: (v) to satisfy, to please; to achieve, to complete.

G

guidance: (n) direction, leadership; advice.
guilty: (adv) having committed an error; worthy of blame; feelings of shame.

H

human rights: (n) the rights of all humans to live free of oppression, fear, etc.
humanity: (n) the human race. All people.
Huqūq Allāh: (n) the Rights of Allāh ﷻ
Huqūq al'Ibād: (n) the Rights of the Worshipers.
hypocrisy: (n) insincerity; saying one thing while doing or feeling the opposite.
hypocrite: (n) one who pratices hypocrisy.

I

inferior: (a) lesser; lower; secondary.
influence: (n) authority; control; to have power over someone.
information: (n) data; knowledge; facts.
intention: (n) aim; goal; purpose; target.
'Injil: (n) The scriptures revealed to the Prophet 'Isa (S).
innocent: (a) blameless; without fault.

J

Jannah: The Garden of Paradise. Heaven.

Jihād: (v) to strive; to struggle. (n) The struggle in the Way of Allāh s.w.t.

K

knowledge: (n) wisdom; learning; intelligence.

L

Law of Equality: (n) right by which the relatives of a murdered person receive fair compensation from the murderer.

M

maintain: (v) to claim, to insist; to keep, to preserve.

Masjid ad-Darar: The masjid of the hypocrites in which they pretended to pray yet were actually plotting against Muslims.

Masjid an-Nabī: The mosque of the Prophet ﷺ in Madīnah.

morals: (n) ethics; the system of honorable beliefs and precepts by which one lives.

Munafiq: (n) hypocrite.

Munāfiqūn: (n) hypocrites. Plural of Munāfiq.

Muttaqī: (n) God-conscious; righteous.

Muttaqūn: plural of Muttaqī.

N

natural: (a) common, normal; of the Earth; unmanufactured.

Nifāq: (n) hypocrisy.

O

oppress: (v) suppress, persecute, tyrannize; to treat unjustly.

oppressor: (n) one who oppresses.

Original Sin: Christian doctrine which states that all humans are born with the sin of Adam.

P

People of the Book: Jews and Christians.

piety: (n) spirituality, respect and devotion for one's religion.

preach: (v) to give a speech in a religious setting; to proclaim; to prescribe moral behavior.

process: (n) manner; means; procedure.

promote: (v) to advance the cause of something; to support someone or something.

protector: (n) one who protects; someone or something which shields from harm.

R

rank: (n) class, level, position; degree.

restrain: (v) to control, to restrict.

retaliation: (n) revenge.

recognize: (v) to know, to identify.

regret: (v) to repent, to feel sorry for having done something; (n) grief, contrition.

repent: (v) to lament, to rue; to ask for Allah's forgiveness with a sincere heart.

resources: (n) riches, assets; means, property, substance.

remind: (v) to cause to remember; to inform; to notify.

relationship: (n) connection; kinship.

righteous: (n) devout, moral; virtuous.

Rope of Allāh: (n) metaphorical term for that bond which unites all Muslims.

S

Shahīd: (n) Martyr for the cause of Allāh ﷻ.

Shaitān: (n) Satan. The devil.

Shūrā: (n) the Islamic concept of mutual consultation for problem solving.

society: (n) community, public; association.

steadfast: (a) constant, faithful, unfailing.

struggle: (v) to fight, to contend.

Sunnah: literally; the Path. The example set by the Prophet Muhammad ﷺ.

superior: (a) exceptional, excellent; better, greater.

support: (v) to sustain; to strengthen. (n) foundation, brace.

T

Taqwā: God- consciousness; fear of Allah ﷻ which guards against wrong action.

Thawab: Spiritual reward given by Allah ﷻ for good deeds and works.

truthful: (a) honest, sincere, earnest.

U

'Ulamā: The scholars of Islām. Its root is the world 'ilm meaning knowledge.

untouchability: (n) The lowest state of the Hindu caste system; an "untouchable" is completely ostrasized from mainstream society by virtue of birth and blodd ties to persons in the lowest of societal levels.

V

verify: (v) to confirm, to make certain about.

W

warmly: (a) affectionately, warmheartedly.

wasteful: (a) extravagant, immoderate, using more than one's proper share.

within: inside.

بِسْمِ اللهِ الرَّحْمَنِ الرَّحِيمِ

Lesson 1

يَا أَيُّهَا ٱلنَّاسُ	O humankind	إِنَّا خَلَقْنَكُم	indeed We created you
مِنْ	from	ذَكَرٍ	(a single pair of) male
وَأُنثَى	and female	وَجَعَلْنَكُم	and We made you
شُعُوبًا وَقَبَائِلَ	nations and tribes	لِتَعَارَفُوا	that you may know each other
إِنَّ أَكْرَمَكُم	truly the most honorable of you	عِنْدَ ٱللَّهِ	in the sight of Allah
أَتْقَكُم	is the most righteous of you	إِنَّ ٱللَّهَ عَلِيمٌ	truly Allah is well-acquainted of all
خَبِيرٌ	All-knowing		

Lesson 2

لَقَدْ	Indeed	خَلَقْنَا	We created
ٱلْإِنسَنَ	the humans	فِي أَحْسَنِ تَقْوِيمٍ	in the best of forms
ثُمَّ رَدَدْنَهُ	then We reduce them		
أَسْفَلَ سَفِلِينَ	to the lowest form		

Lesson 3

أَلَّا	namely	تَزِرُ وَازِرَةٌ	namely that no one shall bean
وِزْرَ أُخْرَى	the burden of another person		
إِلَّا	except	وَأَن لَيْسَ لِلْإِنسَنِ	that a human can have nothing
مَا سَعَى	that for which he makes an effort	وَأَنَّ سَعْيَهُ	and indeed his effort

67

سَوْفَ يُرَىٰ	that shall be seen	ثُمَّ يُجْزَاهُ	then he shall be rewarded
ٱلْجَزَآءَ ٱلْأَوْفَىٰ	for it a full reward		

Lesson 4 _____

إِنَّ ٱللَّهَ لَا يُغَيِّرُ	Indeed ! never will Allah change	مَا بِقَوْمٍ	the condition of a people
حَتَّىٰ يُغَيِّرُواْ	unless they change it	مَا بِأَنْفُسِهِمْ	from within themselves

Lesson 5 _____

وَتَعَاوَنُواْ	And help each other	عَلَى ٱلْبِرِّ	in goodness
وَٱلتَّقْوَىٰ	and piety	وَلَا تَعَاوَنُوٓاْ	and don't cooperate
عَلَى ٱلْإِثْمِ	in sin	وَٱلْعُدْوَٰنِ	and aggression

Lesson 6 _____

لَا إِكْرَاهَ	There is no compulsion	فِى ٱلدِّينِ	in religion
قَد تَّبَيَّنَ	it is made clear	ٱلرُّشْدُ	the right path
مِنَ ٱلْغَيِّ	from error		

Lesson 7 _____

وَهُوَ ٱلَّذِى	He it is who	جَعَلَكُمْ	has appointed you as
خَلَـٰئِفَ ٱلْأَرْضِ	viceroys of the Earth	وَرَفَعَ	And has exalted
بَعْضَكُمْ فَوْقَ بَعْضٍ	some of you over others	دَرَجَتٍ	in status
لِيَبْلُوَكُمْ	that He may try you	فِى مَآ ءَاتَـٰكُمْ	by that which He has given you

Lesson 8

قُلْ	Say	مَنْ حَرَّمَ	who has forbidden
زِينَةَ ٱللَّهِ	the beautiful things of Allah	ٱلَّتِي أَخْرَجَ	that He has produced
لِعِبَادِهِ	for His servants		
وَٱلطَّيِّبَٰتِ مِنَ ٱلرِّزْقِ	and the things clean and pure(which He has provided for sustenance)		

Lesson 9

أَنَّهُ مَن قَتَلَ	That if anyone killed	نَفْسًا	a person
بِغَيْرِ نَفْسٍ	unless it be for murder	أَوْ فَسَادٍ	or for spreading mischief
فِى ٱلْأَرْضِ	in the land	فَكَأَنَّمَا	it would be as if
قَتَلَ	he killed the	ٱلنَّاسَ جَمِيعًا	the whole of humankind
وَمَنْ أَحْيَاهَا	and if anyone saved a life	فَكَأَنَّمَا أَحْيَا	it would be as if he saved the life of

Lesson 10

وَلَكُمْ فِى ٱلْقِصَاصِ	And you have in the law of equality		
حَيَوٰةٌ	(a saving of) life	يَٰأُولِى ٱلْأَلْبَٰبِ	Oh people of understanding
لَعَلَّكُمْ	that you may	تَتَّقُونَ	restrain yourselves

Lesson 11

يَٰأَيُّهَا	Oh you	ٱلَّذِينَ ءَامَنُوا	who believe
ٱتَّقُوا ٱللَّهَ	fear Allah	حَقَّ تُقَاتِهِ	as He should be feared
وَلَا تَمُوتُنَّ	and do not die	إِلَّا وَأَنتُم مُّسْلِمُونَ	unless you are Muslims

Lesson 12

وَمِنَ ٱلنَّاسِ	And among the people	مَن يَقُولُ	are those who say
ءَامَنَّا بِٱللَّهِ	we believe in Allah	وَبِٱلْيَوْمِ ٱلْأَخِرِ	and the last day
وَمَا هُم بِمُؤْمِنِينَ	but they are not of the Believers		

Lesson 13

كُنتُمْ	You are	خَيْرَ أُمَّةٍ	the best community
أُخْرِجَتْ	which has been raised up	لِلنَّاسِ	for humankind
تَأْمُرُونَ	you enjoin	بِٱلْمَعْرُوفِ	what is right
وَتَنْهَوْنَ	and forbid	عَنِ ٱلْمُنكَرِ	from what is wrong
وَتُؤْمِنُونَ بِٱللَّهِ	and you believe in Allah		

Lesson 14

وَٱلْمُؤْمِنُونَ	the Believing men	وَٱلْمُؤْمِنَاتِ	and the Believing women
بَعْضُهُمْ أَوْلِيَاءُ بَعْضٍ	are friends / protectors of one another		
يَأْمُرُونَ	they enjoin	بِٱلْمَعْرُوفِ	the right
وَيَنْهَوْنَ	and forbid	عَنِ ٱلْمُنكَرِ	the wrong
وَيُقِيمُونَ	and they establish	ٱلصَّلَوٰةَ	the Salah
وَيُؤْتُونَ	and they pay	ٱلزَّكَوٰةَ	the Zakah
وَيُطِيعُونَ	and they obey	ٱللَّهَ وَرَسُولَهُ	Allah and his Messanger

Lesson 15 _____

إِنَّمَا ٱلْمُؤْمِنُونَ	Indeed the Believers	إِخْوَةٌ	are one brotherhood
فَأَصْلِحُوا	so make peace	بَيْنَ أَخَوَيْكُمْ	between your brothers
وَٱتَّقُوا ٱللَّهَ	and fear Allah	لَعَلَّكُمْ تُرْحَمُونَ	that you may receive Mercy

Lesson 16 _____

مَنْ عَمِلَ	Whoever works	صَـٰلِحًا	good deeds
مِن ذَكَرٍ	whether male	أَوْ أُنثَىٰ	or female
وَهُوَ مُؤْمِنٌ	and is a Believer	فَلَنُحْيِيَنَّهُ	We will make them live
حَيَوٰةً طَيِّبَةً	a clean and pure life	وَلَنَجْزِيَنَّهُمْ	We will give them
أَجْرَهُمْ	their reward	بِأَحْسَنِ مَا	according to the best
كَانُوا يَعْمَلُونَ	of their action		

Lesson 17 _____

وَلِكُلٍّ وِجْهَةٌ	To each is a goal	هُوَ مُوَلِّيهَا	to which Allah turns him
فَٱسْتَبِقُوا	so strive together	ٱلْخَيْرَاتِ	(for) the good things
أَيْنَ مَا تَكُونُوا	wherever you are	يَأْتِ بِكُمُ ٱللَّهُ	Allah will bring you all
جَمِيعًا	together	إِنَّ ٱللَّهَ	Surely Allah
عَلَىٰ كُلِّ شَىْءٍ قَدِيرٌ	has power over all things		

Lesson 18 _____

| إِنَّمَا ٱلْمُؤْمِنُونَ | Those are true | ٱلَّذِينَ ءَامَنُوا | who have believed |

71

believers in Allah and his Messenger بِٱللَّهِ وَرَسُولِهِ | and never since doubted ثُمَّ لَمْ يَرْتَابُوا

then made Jihad وَجَهَدُوا | their money and their persons بِأَمْوَالِهِمْ وَأَنفُسِهِمْ

in the way of Allah فِى سَبِيلِ ٱللَّهِ | such are the sincere ones أُوْلَـٰئِكَ هُمُ ٱلصَّـٰدِقُونَ

Lesson 19 _____

and those who conduct their affairs with each other وَأَمْرُهُمْ بَيْنَهُمْ | by consultation شُورَىٰ

Lesson 20 _____

Oh you who believe يَـٰأَيُّهَا ٱلَّذِينَ ءَامَنُوا | why do you say لِمَ تَقُولُونَ

that which you do not do مَا لَا تَفْعَلُونَ | most hateful is it كَبُرَ مَقْتًا

in the sight of Allah عِندَ ٱللَّهِ | that you say أَن تَقُولُوا

that which you do not do مَا لَا تَفْعَلُونَ

Lesson 21 _____

Oh Believers يَـٰأَيُّهَا ٱلَّذِينَ ءَامَنُوا | be righteous/ mindful of Allah ٱتَّقُوا ٱللَّهَ

and be وَكُونُوا | with the truthful مَعَ ٱلصَّـٰدِقِينَ

Lesson 22 _____

Say قُلْ | Oh People يَـٰأَهْلَ

of the book ٱلْكِتَـٰبِ | come تَعَالَوْا

إِلَىٰ كَلِمَةٍ سَوَآءٍ to common terms	بَيْنَنَا وَبَيْنِكُمْ between us and you
أَلَّا نَعْبُدَ that we worship none	إِلَّا ٱللَّهَ except Allah
وَلَا نُشْرِكَ بِهِ شَيْئًا we associate no partners with Him	وَلَا يَتَّخِذَ بَعْضُنَا and let none among us take
بَعْضًا أَرْبَابًا others as lords	مِّن دُونِ ٱللَّهِ other than Allah
فَإِن تَوَلَّوْا۟ and if they turn away	فَقُولُوا۟ say
ٱشْهَدُوا۟ Bear witness	بِأَنَّا مُسْلِمُونَ that we are Muslims

Lesson 23 _____

وَلَا تُجَٰدِلُوٓا۟ And do not debate	أَهْلَ ٱلْكِتَٰبِ the People of the Book
إِلَّا بِٱلَّتِي هِىَ أَحْسَنُ except in a beautiful manner	إِلَّا ٱلَّذِينَ unless those who
ظَلَمُوا۟ مِنْهُمْ have done wrong among them	وَقُولُوٓا۟ ءَامَنَّا and say: we believe
بِٱلَّذِىٓ أُنزِلَ إِلَيْنَا in the revelation that came down to us	وَأُنزِلَ إِلَيْكُمْ and in that which came down to you
وَإِلَٰهُنَا our God	وَإِلَٰهُكُمْ وَٰحِدٌ and your God is one
وَنَحْنُ لَهُ مُسْلِمُونَ and it is to Him that we are submitting	

Lesson 24 _____

يَٰٓأَيُّهَا Oh you	ٱلَّذِينَ ءَامَنُوٓا۟ who believe
إِن جَآءَكُمْ فَاسِقٌ if an evil person comes to you	بِنَبَإٍ with news
فَتَبَيَّنُوٓا۟ verify its truth	أَن تُصِيبُوا۟ قَوْمًا in case you harm people
بِجَهَٰلَةٍ unknowingly	فَتُصْبِحُوا۟ and become

عَلَىٰ مَا فَعَلْتُمْ for what you   نَٰدِمِينَ   regretful

Lesson 25 _____

إِنَّمَا يَعْمُرُ He shall build and maintain   مَسَٰجِدَ ٱللَّهِ   the mosques of Allah

مَنْ ءَامَنَ بِٱللَّهِ who believes in Allah   وَٱلْيَوْمِ ٱلْأَخِرِ   and the last day

وَأَقَامَ ٱلصَّلَوٰةَ and offers regular prayer   وَءَاتَى ٱلزَّكَوٰةَ   and gives the Zakah

وَلَمْ يَخْشَ إِلَّا ٱللَّهَ and fears none except Allah

Lesson 26 _____

وَمَا كَانَ ٱلْمُؤْمِنُونَ It was not for the Believers   لِيَنفِرُوا۟ كَآفَّةً   to go forth together

فَلَوْلَا نَفَرَ it would be better   مِن كُلِّ فِرْقَةٍ   of every party

مِنْهُمْ طَآئِفَةٌ only a group should remain   لِيَتَفَقَّهُوا۟   to devote themselves

فِى ٱلدِّينِ to the study of religion   وَلِيُنذِرُوا۟   that they may teach, warn

قَوْمَهُمْ their people   إِذَا رَجَعُوٓا۟ إِلَيْهِمْ   once they return to them

لَعَلَّهُمْ يَحْذَرُونَ that they may learn to guard themselves (against evil)

Lesson 27 _____

وَٱبْتَغِ And seek   فِيمَآ ءَاتَىٰكَ ٱللَّهُ with what Allah has given you

ٱلدَّارَ ٱلْأَخِرَةَ the home of the Hereafter   وَلَا تَنسَ nor forget

نَصِيبَكَ your share   مِنَ ٱلدُّنْيَا in this world

وَأَحْسِن and be kind   كَمَآ أَحْسَنَ ٱللَّهُ إِلَيْكَ as Allah has been

	kind to you		
وَلاَ تَبْغِ ٱلفَسَادَ and seek not mischief	فِى ٱلأَرْضِ	in this land	
إِنَّ ٱللَّهَ لاَ يُحِبُّ for Allah loves not	ٱلـمُفْسِدِينَ	the mischief - makers	

Lesson 28 _____

وَذَكِّرْ	And remind	فَإِنَّ ٱلذِّكْرَىٰ	for reminding
تَنفَعُ	benefits	ٱلـمُؤْمِنِينَ	the Believers